Voices
of Memory 2

Medical Crimes
Medical Experiments in Auschwitz

Published by the International Center for Education
about Auschwitz and the Holocaust

Voices
of Memory 2

Medical Crimes
Medical Experiments in Auschwitz

Irena Strzelecka

Translated by William Brand

Auschwitz-Birkenau State Museum
Oświęcim 2019

This publication was made possible thanks to the financial support from the Foundation for the Commemoration of Victims of Auschwitz-Birkenau Extermination Camp

All documents and photographs included in this publication are to be found in a multimedia presentation available at the following website: www.auschwitz.org

Editors (including the majority of the footnotes, bibliographical notes on prisoners, glossary, and timeline): *Maria Martyniak, Alicja Białecka, Jacek Lachendro, Jacek Lech*

The second corrected version

Translation of German documents: *Jacek Lech*

Cover design: *Robert Płaczek*

Corrections: *Beata Kłos*

Photographs and documents:
Archives of the Auschwitz-Birkenau State Museum in Oświęcim

978-83-7704-024-9

From the Publisher

The International Center for Education about Auschwitz and the Holocaust at the Auschwitz-Birkenau State Museum in Oświęcim is proud to present the first in a series of books that will appear under the joint title *Voices of Memory*. This series arose as a response to requests, which we have frequently received from participants in the specialist seminars and conferences that we have organized at the Museum over the last ten years, for additional source material. Several thousand people have attended various kind of courses, postgraduate programs, and conferences. Many of them want to continue learning about the tragic history of Auschwitz, the Nazi German death camp, and, in the case of teachers, to share this knowledge with their students.

Each of these books is devoted to one of the numerous issues in the complicated history of this camp, and contains, in addition to a scholarly article discussing the subject in detail, a selection of source material from the archives of the Auschwitz-Birkenau State Museum in Oświęcim. These include German records created in the various offices of the Nazi state and the departments in the camp, as well as a rich collection of photographs. For the historian, this material is a priceless source of information and, in the case of some issues, the only source making it possible to learn the truth about the camp, since the camp authorities deliberately falsified certain events in the official records. This applies to the execution of prisoners in the camp, and matters connected with organizing the mass killing of Jews. In such cases, eyewitness accounts of these events are the only way of learning the truth.

The accounts presented in this volume are the testimony of specific people known to us by name, which is all the more reason to remember that the tragedy of Auschwitz is, at one and the same time, the tragedy of the more than one million victims, and also the tragedy of each individual person.

We hope that the publication of the series Voices of Memory will help readers to grasp more fully the uniqueness of the Auschwitz camp, its complicated history, and the contemporary significance of this place for Europe and for the world.

Krystyna Oleksy
Director of the International Center for Education
about Auschwitz and the Holocaust

Historical Outline

Medical Experiments in Auschwitz

German physicians–those at the head of the central SS and Wehrmacht medical organizations, together with the lower-ranking medical personnel under their command, as well as the faculty of research institutes and medical schools with their distinguished academic titles–played an active role in Nazi extermination plans. Ignoring the basic tenets of medical ethics, often at their own initiative, they put their skills at the service of National Socialist ideology despite being fully aware of its criminal aims.

The SS physicians serving in the concentration camps, among them in Auschwitz, played a special role. Violating the Hippocratic oath, they participated in the mass extermination of the Jews, carried out the selection of newly arrived Jewish transports, and oversaw the killing process. They sentenced the most seriously ill and overworked prisoners in the camp hospitals to death in the gas chambers or killed them with lethal phenol injections to the heart, and then deliberately falsified their death certificates. They carried out medical experiments on prisoners and made a mockery of the medical profession in a variety of other ways. By supporting the extermination program in the camp, they earned themselves a place in history as medical criminals.

The participation of numerous German physicians in criminal medical experiments on concentration camp prisoners was a particularly drastic instance of the trampling of medical ethics. The initiators and facilitators of these experiments were Reichsführer SS Heinrich Himmler, together with SS-Obergruppenführer Ernst Grawitz[1], the chief physician of the SS and police, and SS-Standartenführer Wolfram Sievers, the secretary general of

---

[1] Ernst Robert von Grawitz, medical school professor, member of the NSDAP and SS. Former chief physician of the SS and head of the SS Main Sanitary Office, while also head of the German Red Cross. Committed suicide in April 1945.

the Ahnenerbe [Ancestral Heritage] Association and director of the Waffen SS Military-Scientific Research Institute. The SS-WVHA (SS Main Economic and Administrative Office, in charge of concentration camps from March 1942) had administrative and economic authority. Support in the form of specialized analytical studies came from the Waffen SS Hygiene Institute, directed by SS-Oberführer Joachim Mrugowsky, an MD and professor of bacteriology at the University of Berlin Medical School.

Experiments were planned at the highest levels to meet the needs of the army (some were intended to improve the state of soldiers' health) or postwar plans (including population policy), or to reinforce the bases of racial ideology (including advancing views as to the superiority of the "Nordic race").

Aside from experiments planned at the highest levels, many Nazi doctors experimented on prisoners on behalf of German pharmaceutical companies or medical institutes. Others did so in pursuit of their personal interests, or to advance their academic careers.

During the Second World War, Nazi doctors pandered to the expectations of the Third Reich leadership by supporting the regime's demographic policies. They initiated wide-ranging research on methods of mass sterilization that would be applied to peoples regarded as belonging to a lower category. They intended to sterilize both Jews and Slavs, as is shown by the surviving correspondence and postwar testimony of such high-ranking Nazi officials as Viktor Brack, the head of Hitler's chancellery; Karl Brandt, the medical school professor who was Hitler's personal physician and Reich commissar for health and sanitation; Adolf Pokorny, a physician; Rudolf Brandt, a legal scholar who was a personal adviser to Himmler; and Rudolf Höss[2], the commandant of Auschwitz. At the same time as they embarked on the mass murder of the Jews in the gas chambers, they were planning to sterilize the Slavs and the small numbers of Germans with "mixed" Jewish blood, the so-called *Mischlingen.*

Himmler's staff discussed mass sterilization at a secret conferences in 1941, attended by Himmler himself and other leading SS officials, including the chief SS physician, Dr. Ernst Grawitz. They debated about the best method for sterilizing vast numbers of people in the shortest possible time, using the simplest possible methods.

A conference (July 7/8, 1942) attended by Himmler, Professor Karl Gebhardt, and Richard Glücks (the inspector of concentration camps) entrusted

---

[2] Rudolf Höss, commandant of Auschwitz from May 5, 1940 to November 11, 1943, after which he was head of Office Group DI in the SS-WVHA, from where he was seconded to Auschwitz as commander of the SS garrison; in charge of the killing of Hungarian Jews from May 11 to July 26, 1944. On April 2, 1947, the Supreme National Tribunal in Warsaw sentenced him to death. The sentence was carried out in Oświęcim on April 16, 1947.

the search for the desired method of sterilization to Professor Carl Clauberg, an authority in the tretment of infertility who had attended international conferences of gynecologists, and worked during the war as head of the department of women's diseases at the hospital in Chorzów (then Königshütte, Germany).

Himmler responded to requests from Clauberg by ordering him to carry out sterilization experiments at the concentration camp in Oświęcim. Clauberg set to work in barrack no. 30, part of the hospital complex in the women's camp (sector BIa) in Birkenau, at the end of 1942. In April 1943, following orders from above, Rudolf Höss put part of block no. 10 in the main camp at Clauberg's disposal. Between 150 and 400 Jewish women from various countries were held in two upstairs rooms with their windows boarded up because they overlooked the "Death Wall" in the courtyard of block no. 11.[3] The labor office listed these women as "prisoners for experimental purposes" (*Häftlinge für Versuchszwecke*). Most of Clauberg's subjects were women who had already given birth, and who had not stopped menstruating in the camp.

Clauberg developed a method of non-surgical mass sterilization. Under the pretext of performing a gynecological examination, he first checked to make sure that the Fallopian tubes were open, and then introduced a specially prepared chemical irritant, which caused acute inflammation. This led to the obstruction of the tubes. X-rays were used to check the results of each procedure.

Clauberg's accomplices were Johannes Goebel (Göbel), a Ph.D. in chemistry who was the representative of the Schering Werke and the discoverer of the chemical solution that Clauberg used, and an SS orderly named Binning. His medical and nursing staff consisted mostly of female Jewish prisoners. The head physician of block no. 10 from September 1943, with the status of block supervisor, was the gynecological surgeon Alina Białostocka (who went by the name Brewda in camp), a Jewish woman from Poland.

These procedures were carried out in a brutal way. Complications were frequent, including peritonitis and hemorrhages from the reproductive tract, leading to high fever and sepsis. Multiple organ failure and death frequently followed. While some of Clauberg's Jewish patients died in this way, others were deliberately put to death so that autopsies could be carried out.

Clauberg provided Himmler with regular updates on his experiments. On June 7, 1943, he wrote: "The method for the non-surgical sterilization of women that I have developed is now almost perfected (…). As for the questions directed to me by the Reichsführer as to when it will be possible to sterilize 1,000 women in this way, I can give the following answer today, according to the forecasts: if my research continues to yield the results it

---

[3]   The Museum Archives contain several accounts by Polish women prisoners experimented on by Clauberg.

has yielded so far, and there is no reason to believe that this will not be the case, then it will be possible to report in a short time that one experienced doctor in a suitably equipped office and with the help of 10 auxiliary personnel will most probably be able to carry out the sterilization of several hundred, or even a thousand women per day."

In May 1944, Clauberg's experimental station was moved to block no. 1 in the women's camp in the so-called "camp extension" (*Schutzhaftlager-erweiterung*). While continuing his sterilization experiments, Clauberg also prepared to conduct trials of artificial insemination. He and Dr. Goebel also experimented with new radiological markers to be used in the sterilization experiments. Clauberg traveled to Ravensbrück in January 1945, where he continued his experiments on Jewish women prisoners transferred there from Auschwitz, and on Roma women.

In November 1942 (at almost the same time as Clauberg), SS-Sturmbann-nführer Horst Schumann, a Luftwaffe lieutenant and a physician, began his own sterilization experiments at Auschwitz under orders from Victor Brack. Schumann was the former head of the institution for the "incurably ill" at Grafeneck hospital in Wurtemberg and at Sonnenstein, after which he became a member of a special "medical commission" that selected sick and overworked concentration camp prisoners for the gas chambers. Like Clauberg, Schumann was searching for the best method of mass sterilization, which would allow the leaders of the Third Reich to carry out the biological destruction of conquered peoples through "scientific means," by depriving them of their reproductive capacity. According to Höss, Himmler accompanied Schumann's arrival in Auschwitz with an order that he be provided with the required number of male and female prisoners, and all possible assistance.

Schumann moved into barracks no. 30 in the Birkenau women's camp (sector BIa), where an "x-ray sterilization" station had been equipped with two Siemens x-ray machines, so called "*Rentgenbombe*", connected by cables to a lead-shielded control cabin where Schumann could run the machines. Jewish men and women prisoners in groups of several dozen at a time were regularly brought in from the Birkenau camp (and sometimes from block no. 10 in the Main Camp) and subjected to sterilization experiments consisting of the exposure of the women's ovaries and the men's testicles to x-rays. Searching for the optimum radiation dose for achieving complete infertility, Schumann experimented with different doses at different intervals. The prisoners involved in these experiments were generally sent back to work, despite the fact that the x-rays left them with severe radiation burns on the abdomen, groin, and buttocks, and suppurating lesions that resisted healing. Complications led to numerous deaths. Some of the experimental subjects were sent to the gas chambers during selection in the camp.

In the second stage of the experiments, after the passage of several weeks, samples of semen were collected from some of the male prisoners in the Main Camp hospital and examined for the presence and motility of sperm. Additionally, some of Schumann's male and female experimental subjects had their testicles or ovaries removed surgically (unilaterally or bilaterally) for laboratory examination and in order to obtain histological samples. These operations were carried out, often with Schumann present, in block no. 21 (the surgical ward) or blocks nos. 10 and 28 of the Main Camp, as well as in the hospital camp (sector BIIf) in Birkenau. These operations were usually carried out by prisoner physicians, including a Pole, Dr. Władysław Dering[4] (released from the camp in 1944 and employed in Clauberg's private clinic), and a Jew, Dr. Maximilian Samuel (who was put to death in the camp). Some of the prisoners who underwent these operations died of infections or internal hemorrhages.

The results of the experiments on sterilization by x-ray were disappointing. In April 1944, Schumann sent Himmler a report on his Auschwitz experiments titled *On the Effect of X-Rays on the Human Reproductive Glands*, in which he concluded that surgical sterilization was quicker and more reliable. Nevertheless, Schumann continued his experiments at Ravensbrück, beginning that same month.

Only a small portion of the victims of Clauberg and Schumann's experiments survived Auschwitz. The rest died there, receiving lethal injections of phenol or being selected for the gas chambers.

Schumann's x-ray apparatus was removed from Auschwitz in December 1944. The Czech prisoner Stanisław Ślezak, who had installed and operated it, was classified as a "bearer of secrets" (*Geheimnisträger*), transferred to Mauthausen the following month, and shot there.

While Clauberg and Schumann were busy with experiments designed to develop methods for the biological destruction of people regarded by the Nazis as undesirable, another medical criminal, SS-Hauptsturmführer Josef Mengele,[5] was researching the issues of twins and the physiology and pathology of dwarfism. He was also interested in people with different colored irises (*heterochromia iridii*), and in the etiology and treatment of

---

4   Dr. Władysław Dering, gynecologist-obstetrician deported to Auschwitz on August 15, 1940 and employed in the camp hospital. On orders from Horst Schumann he sterilized prisoners surgically. Dering was released on parole from Auschwitz in January 1944. Clauberg hired him at his private clinic in Königshütte (now Chorzów). Dering emigrated to the UK after the war, where he became the object of an investigation and was held in prison for a year and a half before being released for lack of evidence. He died in 1965.

5   Mengele cooperated in his experiments with the Kaiser Wilhelm Institute of Anthropology, Heredity, and Eugenics in Berlin-Dahlem, directed by Prof. Ottmar Freiherr von Verscheur.

the gangrenous disease of the face known as noma (*cancrum oris, gangrenous stomatitis*), a little understood disease endemic to the Gypsy prisoners in Auschwitz.

One of Dr. Mengele's experimental laboratories was located on the grounds of the Gypsy family camp, in the bathhouse that stood next to barrack no. 32. Early in his time at Auschwitz, Mengele was camp physician in the Gypsy camp. After the reorganization of Auschwitz in November 1943, he was named chief camp physician of Auschwitz II-Birkenau Concentration Camp. At the beginning of Mengele's experimentation, his subjects were Gypsy children supplied to him from the so-called "Kindergarten" located in barracks nos. 29 and 31. Before long, he was picking out twins and people with unusual physical characteristics (including the growth disorders expressed in dwarfism and gigantism) during the selection of Jewish transports sent to Auschwitz for extermination. He also found subjects in the family camp for Jews from the Theresienstadt ghetto (sector BIIb) and in camp BIII, known as "Mexico," where Hungarian Jewish women were held when there were too many incoming transports for selection on the ramp to keep pace.

After the liquidation of the Gypsy family camp, Dr. Mengele's experimental subjects were housed in barrack no. 15, in the men's hospital camp (sector BIIf), and in designated hospital barracks in the women's camp.

In the first phase, Dr. Mengele and his medical-nursing staff, chosen from among prisoners with varying sorts of medical backgrounds, experimented on twins and people with inherited anomalies using a wide range of specialist medical techniques: anthropometric (involving the use of precision instruments to measure their height and the length and width of their heads, noses, hands, shoulders, and feet), morphological (analyzing their blood and performing cross-transfusions), radiological, dental, laryngological, oculistic, and surgical. These examinations lasted for hours. Some of them were painful and exhausting—an arduous experience for the terrified, hungry children who predominated among the twins at Mengele's disposal.

The prisoners and the other experimental subjects were photographed, fingerprinted, and had plaster casts taken of their jaws and teeth. On Mengele's orders, the prisoner Dina Gottliebova (from the Theresienstadt family camp sector BIIb) made comparative drawings of their heads, ears, noses, mouths, hands, and feet. All the experimental documentation was filed in individual folders for each subject. Jewish prisoners—Rudolf Vitek (known in Auschwitz as Weiskopf) and a world-famous pediatrician, Dr. Bertold Epstein of the University of Prague—wrote up Mengele's experimental findings.

As soon as the results of the examination of a given dwarf or set of twins had been written up, Dr. Mengele ordered them killed by lethal injection of phenol to the heart, so that he could proceed to the next stage of his experimentation: the autopsy, featuring the comparative analysis of the internal organs. In cases assigned by Mengele, Dr. Jancu Vexler did the autopsy in an autopsy room on the grounds of the Gypsy camp, and later in the sector BIIf hospital camp, and then wrote up the scientific findings. From June 1944, Hungarian Jewish pathologist, Miklos Nyiszli, performed the autopsies in a modern facility in crematorium II. In his memoirs, Dr. Nyiszli wrote that "these experiments–under the cloak of medical research– were performed *in vivo*, that is, on a living organism. They are far from exhausting the problem of twinship from a scientific point of view. They are relative. They do not tell us much. Therefore, they are followed by the next and most important stage of the research–analysis conducted on the basis of the autopsy. The comparison of normal, pathologically developed, or diseased organs. For this to occur, however, a corpse is needed. Since the autopsy and the analysis of the various organs must be carried out simultaneously, the twins must die simultaneously. And so they die simultaneously in the experimental barrack in the Auschwitz camp. We have to do here with a case unprecedented in medicine, two twins dying at the same moment." Anatomical samples that were interesting from a scientific point of view were conserved and sent to the Institute in Berlin-Dahlem for further examination. In order to ensure that they arrived promptly and in good condition, they were stamped "Urgent shipment for important military purposes."[6]

A ward for several dozen Gypsies suffering from noma was set up in part of block no. 22 on the grounds of the Gypsy family camp. As the disease progressed, the patients lost flesh from the soft tissues of the cheek, until the teeth, gums, and jawbone were exposed. Noma sufferers, some of whom were children, received periodical pharmacological treatment and were put on a special high-nutrition diet. Dr. Mengele visited the ward frequently, examining and photographing the Gypsies in stages of the disease that interested him. On his orders, the Czech prisoner Vladimir Zlamar depicted their faces in paintings. Mengele also ordered that selected Gypsy children suffering from Noma be put to death and their corpses sent to the Hygiene Institute in Rajsko for histopathological examination. Samples of individual organs were prepared, and sometimes even complete children's heads conserved in jars.

The laboratory where Mengele carried out his research on heredity operated until the moment of the final evacuation of the camp on January 17, 1945. Mengele left that day, taking his research documentation with him.

---

[6] Miklos Nyiszli, *Pracownia doktora Mengele. Wspomnienia lekarza z Oświęcimia*, Warsaw 1966, p. 43.

Prisoners were also put to death for research purposes in connection with diseases resulting from the effects of starvation on the human organization, particularly "brown liver atrophy" (*braune Atrophie*). A professor of anatomy from the University of Münster who lectured there on anatomy, SS-Obersturmführer Johann Paul Kremer, carried out this research with the consent of SS-Standortarzt Eduard Wirths, the head of the Auschwitz medical service. Kremer lectured on anatomy and heredity in Münster, and held both Ph.D. and MD degrees. He was seconded to Auschwitz from an SS hospital in Prague as the replacement for Dr. Bruno Kitt. Kremer was a camp physician from August 30 to November 18, 1942. He had difficulty finding the proper place to carry out his research. Every morning, at the outpatient clinic in block no. 28 in the Main Camp, he reviewed the prisoners applying for admission to the hospital. Among them were many extremely starved and exhausted prisoners (so called "*Muselmänner*"), the majority of whom were put to death by lethal injection of phenol. From among them and the patients in the hospital, Kremer chose prisoners who struck him as suitable research subjects. Just before putting them to death, as they lay on the autopsy table, he asked them for information he regarded as important, such as their weight before arrest, or the last medicine they had taken. In some cases, these prisoners were photographed. Samples of the liver, spleen, and pancreas were removed while the corpse was still warm and set aside for Kremer. When he left Auschwitz in November 1942 to return to his duties in Münster, Kremer took the photographs of his victims and these samples with him.

From 1941 to 1944, the camp SS physicians Friedrich Entress, Helmuth Vetter, Eduard Wirths, and to a lesser extent Fritz Klein, Werner Rhode, Hans Wilhelm König, Victor Capesius (head of the camp pharmacy), and Bruno Weber (director of the SS Hygiene Institute in Rajsko) used Auschwitz prisoners in tests of the tolerance and effectiveness of new medical preparations or drugs designated by the code names B-1012, B-1034, B-1036, 3582, and P-111. They also used prisoners as experimental subjects in tests of the drugs Rutenol and Periston, which had not yet been put into general use. The SS medical personnel were acting on behalf of IG Farbenindustrie, and mostly of Bayer, which was a part of IG Farbenindustrie. These drugs were given in various forms (pills, granules, liquid, intravenous, injection, and liquid suppositories) and doses to prisoners suffering from such contagious diseases as trachoma, typhus, tuberculosis, diphtheria, and erysipelas. In many cases, the prisoners were first deliberately infected with these diseases. Pharmaceutical experiments were carried out in the hospital blocks of the Main Camp (mostly in the contagious diseases ward), the camp in Birkenau, and the camp hospital in Monowice. The prisoners involved in these experiments underwent regular x-rays and had samples taken for laboratory analysis. If they died, autopsies were performed to ascertain any effects of the drugs on internal organs. The prisoner physicians Władysław Tondos, Władysław Fejkiel, and Stanisław Kłodziński worked in the camp hospital and witnessed these trials. They stated that the drugs given to the prisoners had no therapeutic effect. They did, however, cause digestive symptoms including bloody vomiting, painful bloody diarrhea containing flecks of mucous membranes, and impairment of the circulatory system. Kłodziński stated that 50 people suffering from typhus were treated with the preparation designated „3582"; 15 of them died. Of 75 prisoners treated for tuberculosis with Rutenol, 40 died.[7]

Dr. Władysław Tondos, head of a tuberculosis sanatorium in Zakopane before his arrest, stated after the war that "Dr. Helmut Vetter appeared at the concentration camp in Oświęcim as an SS physician in 1942. Prisoner physicians knew him before the war, when Vetter had traveled around Poland as a representative of Bayer promoting that firm's products. After his arrival [in Auschwitz – I.S.], previously unknown preparations began to be applied. In order to test these products, healthy prisoners were infected with blood from typhus sufferers, injecting 5 [c.c.] of blood intravenously. These deliberately infected people were then treated with the new preparations. These were products from the Bayer company. On the basis of observations, we noted that these preparations were ineffective against typhus, and the majority of the patients died."[8]

Capesius, Weber, and Rhode carried out pharmacological experiments in which they administered an unknown narcotic substance, with the same color and smell as coffee, to prisoners. Several prisoners died as a result. The substance was intended for administration to prisoners of war, in order to make them divulge military secrets.

SS physicians Helmuth Vetter and Friedrich Entress subjected several dozen Auschwitz prisoners to experiments designed to define precisely the incubation period of typhus and determine when the blood of typhus patients is most contagious, and when it ceases to be contagious. Here, too, the SS physicians deliberately infected healthy prisoners through infusions of the blood of typhus sufferers. They tested the effectiveness of an unknown typhus vaccine on sick prisoners. These procedures caused numerous complications in prisoners who were already seriously ill and badly exhausted.

Aside from his pharmacological experiments, Dr. Eduard Wirths also attempted to boost the scientific career of his younger brother, a gynecologist from Hamburg, by joining him from the spring of 1943 in experiments

---

[7] APMA-B (Archives of the Auschwitz-Birkenau State Museum in Oświęcim), *Trial of the Auschwitz Garrison*, vol. 59, pp. 53–67; APMAB, D-AuI-5, inventory no. 29713, 29714. Various reports on the hospital.

[8] APMA-B, *Höss Trial Collection*, vol. 7, pp. 78–79.

on cervical cancer. Subjects were chosen from among the Jewish women prisoners held upstairs in block no. 10 in the main camp. The women were examined there for signs of pre-cancerous changes in the cervix. When they identified or suspected such changes, they removed the cervix and sent samples to a histological laboratory in Hamburg. In some cases, Wirths ordered prisoners from the political department studio to photograph the procedure. After a certain time, the experimental subjects were sent to the women's camp in Birkenau.

In the late summer of 1944, the Wehrmacht sent Emil Kaschub, a physician with the rank of corporal, to Auschwitz in an effort to unmask the various methods of malingering that were becoming widespread among German soldiers, especially on the eastern front. These methods included self-inflicted wounds, abscesses, fever, and infectious hepatitis. Kaschub experimented on Jewish prisoners by rubbing various toxic substances into their skin or injecting them into their limbs, and giving them oral medicine (Atebrine) in order to provoke the same symptoms being presented by German soldiers. Kaschub carried out his experiments in an isolated, heavily guarded room upstairs in block no. 28 in the main camp.

Samples of pus and skin along with the underlying tissue were sent for analysis at the VIII sanitary district in Wrocław. This effort to expose Wehrmacht malingerers and shirkers came at the price of the suffering and permanent injury of dozens of young Jewish prisoners, in whom Kaschub induced inflammations, suppurating sores, and abscesses that refused to heal and resulted in gangrene. Some of these subjects were sent to the gas chambers during selection in the camp hospital.

In 1942, SS-Hauptsturmführer August Hirt, a professor and head of the department of anatomy at the Reich University in Strasbourg, set about assembling a collection of Jewish skeletons under the auspices of the Ahnenerbe Foundation. Himmler gave him permission to choose as many prisoners in Auschwitz as he needed. The selection of 115 prisoners (79 Jewish men, 30 Jewish women, 2 Poles, and 4 "Asiatics" – probably Soviet POWs) and the initial "processing" of them was carried out by SS-Hauptsturmführer Bruno Beger, who held a doctorate and worked with the Military Scientific-Research Institute of the Ahnenerbe Foundation. Beger came to Auschwitz in the first half of 1943. The initial "processing" consisted of taking anthropometric measurements of the prisoners and collecting personal information about them. This work lasted until June 15, 1943. After going through quarantine, some of the prisoners chosen by Berger were sent in July and early August to Natzweiler-Struthof concentration camp, where they were put to death in the gas chambers. Their corpses were sent to Hirt for use in his collection of skeletons, which was intended to facilitate anthropological studies demonstrating the supremacy of the "Nordic race."

On November 27, 1944, a group of 20 Jewish children were sent from Auschwitz to Neuengamme concentration camp and put at the disposal of Dr. Kurt Heissmeyer, who was conducting research on tuberculosis. In April 1945, these children were hanged from the heating pipes in a school on Bullenhuserdamm in Hamburg. Prisoner physicians who knew the inside story about Heissmeyer's experiments were hanged along with them.

The Auschwitz medical experiments surely include, as well, the operations carried out by SS physicians Friedrich Entress, Horst Fischer and Heinz Thilo, who did not possess qualifications as surgeons. The operations were completely unnecessary from the medical point of view, and were only carried out for practice. Other procedures carried out for training purposes included inducing pneumothoraces (collapsed lungs) in prisoners with tuberculosis, and performing spinal taps on prisoners with meningitis. Accounts and memoirs by former prisoners also include descriptions of other sorts of experiments, the purposes of which cannot be established.

The prisoners were already living under conditions that were extreme in every imaginable way, and these experiments were a death sentence for many of them. The fate of their experimental subjects was a matter of indifference for the SS physicians. In order to cover their tracks, they often ordered the victims of their experiments killed by lethal injection of phenol to the heart, or in the gas chambers.

Selected Sources

Carl Clauberg

Born in Wupperhoff on September 18, 1898. MD, gynecologist, professor at Königsberg (Kaliningrad) University. During the war, he was director of the Women's Disease Clinic at St. Hedwig's Hospital in Königshütte (Chorzów). From the end of 1942 to January 1945, on the orders of Reichsführer SS Heinrich Himmler, he carried out sterilization experiments on Jewish women prisoners in Auschwitz. After the war, he remained in Soviet captivity until October 1955, when he settled in West Germany. On November 21 of that year, he was arrested, stripped of all his academic titles, and disbarred from medical practice by the German medical association. During preparations for his trial, he died in prison in Kiel on August 9, 1957.

Carl Clauberg. Photo at right taken in prison. (APMA-B, neg. no. 432, 21843).

Experimental block no. 10 on the grounds of the main camp in Oświęcim (Auschwitz I).

Block no. 10. Room, where women prisoners subjected to experiments were hospitalized, Postwar photo.

Barracks no. 30, no longer standing, in the women's camp (sector BIa) in Birkenau. (APMA-B, neg. no. 10336).

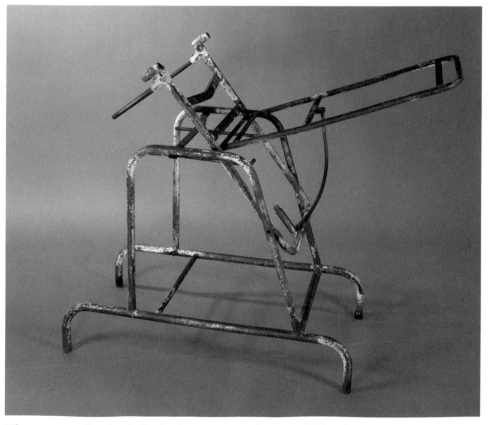

The gynecological chair from experimental block no. 10.

Der Reichsführer-SS

Reichsarzt SS

II/98/41.

332/13

Berlin, den 29. Mai 1941.

Betr.: Unfruchtbarmachung von Frauen.

Bezug: Vortrag beim Reichsführer-SS am 27.5.41.

An den

Reichsführer-SS H. H i m m l e r ,

B e r l i n SW 11

Prinz Albrechtstr. 8.

Reichsführer !

Bei der am 27.5.41 im Beisein von Herrn Professor
Clauberg stattgefundenen Besprechung über dessen neue
Methode zur operationslosen Unfruchtbarmachung minder-
wertiger Frauen ist leider ein Missverständnis unter-
laufen:

Prof. Clauberg benötigt zur Ausarbeitung der Methode
die hierfür bereitzustellenden Frauen bei sich in seiner
eigenen Klinik in Königshütte oder in der Nähe,

   da die Methode sich noch in der Ausarbeitung befindet,

    da Prof. Clauberg hierfür seinen eigens dazu beschafften
    klinischen Apparat an Ort und Stelle benötigt und

    bei Zwischenfällen jederzeit zu Operationen persön-
    lich zur Verfügung stehen muss.

Eine nochmalige eingehende Aussprache mit Prof. Clauberg
hat ergeben, dass unter diesen Umständen eine Durchführung der Versuchsarbeiten in Ravensbrück nicht in Frage
kommen kann.

Bei der unerhörten Bedeutung, die ein solches Verfahren
im Sinne einer negativen Bevölkerungspolitik haben würde
und der daraus sich ergebenden Wichtigkeit, eine einwandfreie Ausarbeitung der Methode mit allen Mitteln zu för-

- 2 -

**Document in which SS physician general (Reichsarzt SS) Dr. Ernst
Grawitz requests Himmler's permission to set up a research institute
for Clauberg.** (APMA-B, neg.no. 435/Λ).

Translation:

Berlin, May 29, 1941

Reichsführer SS
Reichsarzt SS

Subject: Sterilization of women
Reference to: Report at the office of the Reichsführer SS on May 27, 1941

To:
Reichsführer SS, Heinrich Himmler
Berlin SW 11
Prinz Albrechstr. 8

Reichsführer!

During the meeting of May 27, 1941 in the presence of Prof. Clauberg on the subject of his new method of non-surgical sterilization of women who are defective in racial terms, the following misunderstanding arose:

For the development of the above method for this purpose, Prof. Clauberg must have women at his disposal in his own clinic in Köningshütte [now Chorzów – I.S.] or in the vicinity, since he must have the apparatus that he constructed for this purpose there. Also, in case of any incidents, he must always be present to perform an operation if needed.

A new, thoroughgoing discussion with Prof. Clauberg indicates that, under the present circumstances, the experimental work cannot be carried out in Ravensbrück.

In view of the unparalleled importance that this method takes on within the framework of negative population policy, and the resulting importance of giving the fullest possible support to the best possible development of this method, I permit myself, Herr Reichsführer, to propose the creation for Prof. Clauberg of a research institute in Königshütte or in the vicinity, with an affiliated concentration camp for about 10 persons.

In case of your consent, I ask to be given the authority to conduct further negotiations in your name with SS-Gruppenführer Pohl and SS-Brigadeführer Glücks.

E. Grawitz
(illegible signature)

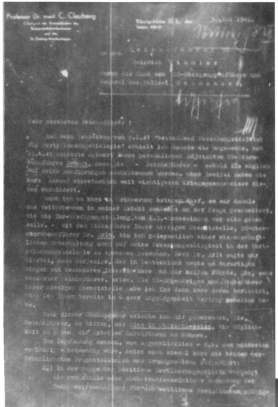

Document in which Clauberg presents the scope and organization of the institute he envisions. His plans call for the use of women prisoners for experimental purposes. (APMA-B, neg. no. 437/A).

Second page of the letter in which Clauberg outlines the scope of his planned institute.

Translation:

(...)

After consultation, I make bold, Reichsführer, obediently to request permission to conduct this work <u>here in Upper Silesia</u>.

The most urgent tasks and basic problems may be recapitulated once again at this point as a way of indicating what is needed at present, in other words, at least temporarily:

A.) In the question of positive population policy, the possible or highly probable significance of the tilling of the soil requires an explanation of the female capacity for reproduction. This must be studied experimentally and scientifically considered on animals at first (on the proverbially most fertile experimental animal, with the greatest variation in fertility–the rabbit). The question is whether good general nutrition achieved as a result of the food produced by intensive agriculture might lower fertility, and if so, which factors (positive or negative) are responsible for this.

B.) In regard to the issue of negative population policy, there is now a situation in which it is necessary to shift from experiments on animals (in which I have seen possibilities for non-surgical sterilization) to the first experiments on humans.

For this purpose, the following are necessary:

Re: A.) <u>The problem of fertility and the tilling of the soil</u>

1.) Land–as far as possible, "virgin," "wild," or previously "poorly" managed. At least <u>10 *morgs*</u> will be needed for the initial experiments on animals.

2.) Personnel to tend the soil.

3.) Animal material–that is, several hundred female rabbits, and also the corresponding, necessary number of rabbits.

4.) Cages and provision for the animals.

5.) Personnel to tend the animals.

Re: B) <u>Non-surgical sterilization</u>

1.) The possibility of accommodation for 5–10 women at a time (single or double rooms), corresponding to the conditions found in hospital rooms.

2.) Special x-ray equipment–apparatus and accessories.

3.) Smaller instruments and auxiliary material.

Reichsführer! Without wanting to anticipate your decision, I permit myself to present a proposal for ordering the conducting of experiments and the installation of equipment necessary for points A and B in the Auschwitz camp; as I mentioned to you in my oral statement, I would willingly subordinate myself to you as the director of a research institute that would function exclusively on the basis of your recommendations.

Der Reichsführer-SS   Dokument Nr.NO-214

   Reichsarzt-SS   Berlin,d n 3o.Mai 1941

Az.: IV/1o2/41.

               Geheime Reichssache.

Betr.: Behandlung weiblicher Unfruchtbarkeit;

Bezug: Vortrag beim Reichsführer-SS am 27.5.41.

An den

Reichsführer-SS - Persönlicher Stab

B e r l i n SW 11

Prinz Albrechtstr.8.

Nachstehend überreiche ich Ihnen eine Aufstellung
der mit der Behandlung weiblicher Unfruchtbarkeit nach
der Methode Prof.Glauberg beauftragten Fachärzte:

    1.) Prof.Glauberg, Königshütte /O.S.,
                      Kneppschaftskrankenhaus,

    2.) SS-Standartenführer Prof.Dr.von Wolff,
                      Berlin W 15, Meineckestr.4.,

    3.) SS-Sturmbannführer Prof.Dr.Erhardt,
                      Granz,Universitäts-Frauenklinik,

    4.) SS-Hauptsturmführer Prof.Dr.M.Guenther K.F.
                      Schulze,Greifswald, Universitäts-
                      Frauenklin k.

                      Der Reichsarzt- SS

                        Grawitz

                  SS-Brigadeführer

(L.d.n.6 k.48 akt procesu

lekarskie o)

List of SS-doctors authorised to carry out treatment of infertility in women using Dr. Clauberg's method.
(APMA-B, neg. no. 436).

Translation:

Document No. NO-214

Reichsführer SS
Reichsarzt SS [SS Physician General]   Berlin, May 30, 1941
Az.: IV/102/41

Secret State Business

<u>Re:</u> Treatment of infertility in women
<u>Reference to:</u> Report at the office of the Reichsführer SS on May 27, 1941

To:
Reichsführer SS – private staff
B e r l i n SW 11
Prinz Albrechtstr. 8

Attached I send you a list of specialist doctors authorized to treat infertility in women using Prof. Clauberg's method.

1.) Prof. Clauberg, Köningshütte / Upper Silesia, Kneppschaftskrankenhaus,
2.) SS-Standartenführer, Prof. Dr. von Wolff, Berlin W 15, Meineckestr. 4,
3.) SS-Sturmbannführer Prof. Dr. Erhardt, Graz, Universität-Frauenklinik,
4.) SS-Hauptsturmführer Prof. Dr. M. Guenther K.F., Schulze, Greifswald, Universität-Frauenklinik.

Reichsarzt SS [SS Physician General]
Grawitz
SS-Brigadeführer

(L.d.n 6 p.48 proceedings of the doctors' trial)

Führer-Hauptquartier, den   Juli 1942.

Geheime Reichssache !

1 Ausfertigung

Am 7.7.1942 hat eine Besprechung stattgefunden zwischen dem Reichsführer-ϟϟ, ϟϟ-Brigadeführer Professor Dr. G e b h a r d t , ϟϟ-Brigadeführer G l ü c k s und ϟϟ-Brigadeführer Professor K l a u b e r g , Königshütte. Inhalt der Besprechung war die Sterilisierung von Jüdinnen. Der Reichsführer-ϟϟ hat dem ϟϟ-Brigadeführer Prof. Klauberg zugesagt, daß ihm für seine Versuche an Menschen und an Tieren das Konzentrationslager Auschwitz zur Verfügung steht. Es sollte anhand einiger Grundversuche ein Verfahren gefunden werden, daß die Sterilisierung bewirkt, ohne daß die Betroffenen davon etwas merken. Sobald das Ergebnis dieser Versuche vorliegt, wollte der Reichsführer-ϟϟ noch einmal einen Bericht vorgelegt bekommen, damit dann an die praktische Durchführung zur Sterilisierung der Jüdinnen herangegangen werden kann.

Ebenso sollte am besten unter Herzuziehung von Professor Dr. H o h l f e l d e r , der ein Röntgenspezialist in Deutschland ist, geprüft werden, in welcher Weise durch Röntgenbestrahlung bei Männern eine Sterilisierung erreicht werden kann.

Der Reichsführer-ϟϟ hat allen beteiligten Herrn gegenüber betont, daß es sich hier um geheimste Dinge handle, die nur intern besprochen werden könnten, wobei jeweils die zu den Versuchen oder Besprechungen Hinzugezogenen auf Geheimhaltung verpflichtet werden müssten.

ϟϟ-Obersturmbannführer.

Note in which Rudolf Brandt, doctor of jurisprudence and personal administrative assistant to Himmler, discusses the result of the meeting with Himmler on sterilization experiments. It indicates that Himmler had given Clauberg permission to carry out experiments on Auschwitz prisoners. (APMA-B, neg. no. 3170).

Translation:

Führer Headquarters, (…)* July 1942

Secret State Business!
No copies

On July 7, 1942 there was a meeting in Königshütte [Chorzów] between the Reichsführer SS, SS-Brigadeführer Prof.Dr.Gebhardt, SS-Brigadeführer Glücks, and SS-Brigadeführer Prof. Klauberg [sic]. The subject of the meeting was the streilization of Jewesses. The Reichsführer SS promised SS-Brigadeführer Prof. Klauberg that Auschwitz Concentration Camp is at his disposal for his experiments on people and animals. With the help of several basic experiments, a method is to be found leading to sterilization, so that the people subjected to this procedure will not notice anything.

After the presentation of the results of these experiments, the Reichsführer SS wishes to obtain a report that will then make it possible to undertake the practical carrying out of the sterilization of Jewesses.

A study should also be made, preferably after the involvement in this matter as a whole of Prof. Dr. Hohlfelder, a specialist in radiology from Germany, of the way in which to achieve the sterilization of men through exposure to x-rays.

The Reichsführer SS stressed to all those present that this is a matter of the most secret issues, which may be discussed only in a closed circle, and that therefore the people involved in the experiments or discussion of this issue must be sworn each time to secrecy.

(signed)
Brandt
SS-Obersturmbannführer

* Date partially illegible

Letter in which Clauberg informs Himmler that the method he has developed can be used to sterilize several hundred up to a thousand women a day. (APMA-B, neg. no. 442).

Second page of the letter in which Clauberg informs Himmler about the number of women who can be sterilized per day with the use of his method.

Translation:

Reichsführer SS   Königshütte, June 7, 1943
(address illegible)

excerpt

SECRET

To:
Reichsführer SS

Herr Heinrich H i m m l e r

B e r l i n

Most Respected Reichsführer!

(…)
The method for the non-surgical sterilization of women that I have developed is now almost perfected. It is performed by way of a one-time injection from the direction of the entrance to the cervix and can be carried out during the standard gynecological examination familiar to every doctor. When I say that this method "is almost ready," this means that:

1.) It only remains to perfect it.

2.) It can already be carried regularly today as part of our standard eugenic sterilization instead of operations, which it can in fact replace.

(…)
As for the questions directed to me by the Reichsführer as to when it will be possible to sterilize 1,000 women in this way, I can give the following answer today, according to the forecasts: if my research continues to yield the results it has yielded so far, and there is no reason to believe that this will not be the case, then it will be possible to report in a short time that one experienced doctor in a suitably equipped office and with the help of 10 auxiliary personnel will most probably be able to carry out the sterilization of several hundred, or even a thousand women per day.

A page from the list of labor assignments for women prisoners in Auschwitz for April 1943. Item no. 10 (*Häftlinge und Pfleger für Versuchszwecke*) **is the number of women assigned for experimental purposes.** (APMA-B, neg. no. 434).

Eilt !

Prof. Dr. med. Carl C l a u b e r g sucht

mehrere tüchtige, weibliche

Schreibmaschinenkräfte

die entweder arbeitslos (was unwahrscheinlich) oder abends in ihrer Freizeit als Ueberstunden für einige Tage, täglich 2 bis 3 Stunden, für mich zu arbeiten in der Lage sind. Zu melden s o f o r t zwischen entweder 9 und 10 Uhr oder 19 und 20 Uhr in der Chirurgischen Universitätsklinik (Privatstation, Zimmer 1), auch Sonntag. Es könnte sein, daß für die beste von ihnen sich die Möglichkeit zu einer Dauerstellung ergibt. In dem Falle: Probezeit, Reise mit mir im Wagen durch Deutschland mit anschließendem Kuraufenthalt (4 Wochen) und während dieser Zeit Arbeit für mich tägl. 2—3 Stunden bei „Alles frei u. Gehalt".

After returning from the Soviet captivity, during which he went unnoticed among the mass of German prisoners, Clauberg appeared on the radio and television as well as placing an advertisement in the press offering employment to several qualified typists. This helped to identify him, and contributed to his arrest on November 21, 1955. (APMA-B, neg. no. 447).

Translation:

URGENT!
Prof. of Medicine Dr. Carl Clauberg seeks
several hard-working
women typists

unemployed (unlikely) or able to work for me evenings or in their spare time after hours for several days, 2–3 hours per day. Apply immediately from 9:00–10:00 or 19:00–20:00 at the University Surgical Clinic (private ward, room no. 1), Sundays included. Permanent positions may become available for the best candidates. In such case, I offer: trial period, travel by train car throughout Germany, followed by stays in spa town (4 weeks), working 2–3 hours per day for me during this time with full room and board in addition to pay.

Excerpt from testimony before the Supreme National Tribunal in Poland (1947) by the former Auschwitz commandant, SS-Obersturmbannführer Rudolf Höss, on Professor Carl Clauberg's sterilization experiments.

It is known to me that medical experiments were conducted on prisoners in the German concentration camps. The initiative came from the doctors, frequently university professors, who were interested in the solution to a given medical problem; they sought subjects in the concentration camps on whom they could experiment and check the results in the areas that interested them. In these matters, they approached Gravitz, who went through Himmler and then the central supervisory authorities to obtain permission for them to conduct their experiments. Dr. Clauberg, a full professor of the university in Königsberg, about 45 years of age, Luftwaffe *Oberleutnant* [senior lieutenant] Dr. Schumann from Hitler's Chancellery (*Kanzlei des Führers*) – both members of the camp garrison[9] – and the camp garrison physician, Dr. Edward Wirths, carried out experiments in Auschwitz. Clauberg was a specialist in gynecology and, during the war, was placed in charge of the women's diseases clinic in Königshütte. He achieved notable results in the treatment of infertile women, and restored their fertility through his treatments. From conversations with Dr. Clauberg I know that, according to his observations, the majority of the cases of female infertility are caused by the adhesion of the Fallopian tubes, which results in their obstruction. To remove these defects, he injected into the Fallopian tubes a liquid that he had invented, which diminished the adhesion of the tubes and opened them up again. Since this procedure produced the desired result and infertile women became pregnant, Clauberg attained renown. Himmler, who attached a great deal of importance to these matters, also learned about these results and achievements. Himmler summoned Clauberg and ordered him to treat and cure the wife of one of the high-ranking SS officials, who was infertile. On this occasion, Himmler suggested to Clauberg the idea of whether his method might be used to achieve the opposite result, that is, to cause infertility in women who were previously fertile, in order to come up with a quick, certain means of sterilization that could be applied on a mass scale. Clauberg took an interest in this matter, sought an appropriate chemical substance, and sent a written report to Himmler, as a result of which Himmler summoned him. After discussing the matter, Himmler told Clauberg that he could conduct these experiments in Auschwitz on the Jewish women prisoners held there. As a result of this handling of the matter, I received an order from Himmler to permit Clauberg to experiment on the Je-

---

[9]   Not in fact officially part of the Auschwitz organizational structure.

wish women imprisoned in the Auschwitz camp, and to give him whatever help he needed. Once Clauberg arrived at the camp, I held a conference with him in which garrison physician Wirths and camp director Aumeier also took part. As a result of this conference, I ordered that block no. 10 be placed at Clauberg's disposal, and ordered the camp director to send the women Clauberg would seek out to that block (…).

Both block no. 10 and, later, Clauberg's new experimental station were strictly isolated; the women prisoners there were not allowed out and men who did not belong to the staff were forbidden to enter. Clauberg himself chose the women on whom he experimented from among the prisoners presented to him for that purpose by camp physician Wirths and the women's camp physician. On the basis of my own observations, I would say that these were women between the ages of 20 and 30. In discussions with me, Clauberg indicated that he was interested in women who had already given birth. This was important to him because he wanted to avoid experimenting on inducing infertility in women who were already infertile for some reason. The second condition that a woman had to fulfill was still to be menstruating (…).

Women were placed in Clauberg's block as if they were being admitted to a hospital. These women were entered in the Arbeitseinsatz records as "prisoners for experimental purposes" (*Häftlinge für Versuchszwecke*). The women in Clauberg's block did not go out to work, but were rather employed at such light work as darning socks, and they received normal camp food. There was an examination room set up in Clauberg's experimental block, a room equipped with x-ray apparatus, and an office. The camp bore the cost of equipping this block with the necessary apparatus, and the camp construction department (*Bauleitung*) carried out the building work. After conducting detailed interviews with the women who were supposed to undergo the procedure, Clauberg placed such a woman in the gynecological chair and, with x-ray monitoring, injected a contrastive mass into her Fallopian tubes in order to check that they were not obstructed. After confirming that the Fallopian tubes were completely unobstructed, the woman got out of the chair and ran around the room for a moment while Clauberg examined the next woman. Then he put the first one back in the gynecological chair and again, with x-ray monitoring, injected into her Fallopian tubes a mixture of a contrasting solution and the liquid that he prepared specially along with his collaborator, the chief chemist of the Schering chemical works (Schering Werke), Gebel. On several occasions, I personally observed Clauberg carrying out this procedure. Clauberg informed me in detail about the way he carried out the procedure and demonstrated it for me, but he never gave me the chemical composition of the substance he used. According to his explanations, this substance caused the adhesion of the Fallopian tubes, and thus their obstruction, within 6 weeks in all cases. (…) In doubtful cases, where shadows appeared in the x-rays, Clauberg repeated the procedure, again injecting the women with that chemical substance but in a more concentrated solution. (…)

Himmler emphasized and attached importance to the search for a means of artificially inducing infertility that would be quick and certain, could be applied inconspicuously (*unauffällig*), and would be suitable for use on a mass scale. (…)

From conversations with Clauberg and the RSHA officials Thomson and Eichmann, I know that Himmler intended to use Clauberg's method to liquidate and biologically destroy the Polish and Czech people. (…)

As Jews, all the victims of his experiments were to be destroyed after the achievement and confirmation of the results. After the liquidation of the Auschwitz camp, these women were transferred to Ravensbrück, where Clauberg intended to continue his research. What happened to them afterwards, I do not know.

Source: APMA-B, Höss Trial Collection, vol. 21, pp. 131–137.

Excerpts from an account by Kazimiera Topór, former prisoner no. 25923, on the sterilization experiments conducted by Nazi doctors Clauberg and Schumann in barrack no. 30 in the Birkenau women's camp (sector BIa).

Dr. Schumann's laboratory in barrack no. 30 was next to Dr. Clauberg's laboratory. Inside the latter was a gynecological table together with a moveable x-ray plate mounted above it (on rails). This apparatus was installed in December 1942. (…)

The women prisoners brought in for experiments had to disrobe in the waiting room, and they were called into the laboratory one at a time. There, after having their x-rays taken with the movable plate, Clauberg used a medical instrument to inject some sort of liquid into their reproductive organs. After the experiments, Clauberg left 6 to 8 prisoners at his disposal in barrack no. 30 and sent the rest back to the camp. He placed these few chosen women in a special room next to his laboratory. In the room, there were metal single beds where these prisoners stayed for a period of a week. They had chills and high temperatures, and suffered delusions. There were even instances of deaths. (…)

After a certain period of time (more than a week), the sick women returned to the camp.

Clauberg's experiments were cloaked in secrecy. Not even the female SS personnel knew what they were about or in general–as I have mentioned above–what was actually happening in barrack no. 30. I did not notice Schumann and Clauberg ever consulting each other.

Source: APMA-B, Statements Collection, vol. 54, pp. 169–175.

Excerpts from testimony at the trial of Rudolf Höss by Felicja Ple-szowska, former prisoner no. 29875, employed as a nurse in experimental blocks nos. 30 (Birkenau sector BIa) and 10 (main camp).

On January 18, 1943, I was deported to Auschwitz concentration camp, where I was placed in the women's camp in Birkenau and obtained prisoner number 29875. That same day, I was assigned at once to labor at the demolition of bombed-out houses about 6 kilometers from the camp. I do not remember the name of the locality where I worked. After four weeks of that work, in February 1943, I was transferred to block no. 30 of the women's camp in Birkenau. I had previously been in block no. 8 of that camp. Block no. 30 was a single-story wooden building. It contained a dentists' office, and next an x-ray station and a room where the crew of Professor Glauberg's [Clauberg's – I.S.][10] experimental station, which was soon to go into operation in the Auschwitz main camp, stayed. I was in block no. 30 until April 3, 1943. Aside from me, there were 6 or 7 other prisoners there, of whom I remember Sylwia Friedmann of Slovakian nationality; Ryja Hans–also Slovakian; Sonia Fischer or Fischman, a German from Vienna; Helena Frank, a Belgian; Ilona Vohrysék, a Czech; and Genowefa Białostocka, a Pole. The [Jewish – I.S.] prisoners I have named and I made up the crew of Clauberg's future experimental station, and we were staying temporarily in block no. 30, waiting for that laboratory in Auschwitz I to go into operation. (…) The SS physician [Horst – I.S.] Schumann, who was called "Professor," as well as Professor Clauberg, worked from time to time in the x-ray office. The latter began his work in December 1942. As I later learned when talking to Doctor Max Samuel, Clauberg was working at the time on finding a substance to induce sterility. Dr. Samuel told me that he already knew about such a substance, and that it had been used in Germany before the war. It was, namely, Iodipine. It was not manufactured in Germany, however, but imported from abroad, and this is why the Germans were trying to find a substitute of their own. Professor Clauberg was one of those working on this. Professor Clauberg had a large clinic in Königshütte, which is where he lived. He only came to Auschwitz from time to time to carry out experiments. Several women prisoners were assigned to Professor Clauberg in December 1942 for his studies. These women lived in block no. 27 in the women's camp at the exclusive disposal of Clauberg. Clauberg injected something into their reproductive organs that was supposed to cause temporary sterility. Next, Clauberg's patients were x-rayed in block no. 30 in order to determine how their organisms were reacting to the injections. At that time, additionally, Schumann, whom I have

---

[10]   Correct spelling used afterwards.

mentioned already, was also carrying out procedures in the x-ray room; he was working on the problem of sterilizing men. He attempted to induce this sterilization through the appropriate exposure of the testicles to x-rays. For this purpose, he was allotted the required number of male prisoners. During the time I spent in block no. 30, he sterilized 100 men. Schumann's procedures were very painful and dangerous to life. There were frequent cases of men dying immediately after such procedures. On April 3, 1943, Clauberg's entire staff was transferred to block no. 10 in the Auschwitz main camp. This was a two-story brick building. It was separated from block no. 11 by the courtyard where the mass shooting of prisoners at the notorious "Death Wall" took place. On the ground floor of block no. 10 were two large hospital rooms referred to as *revirs* [infirmaries], the x-ray station, an operating room, a dentist's office, the hygiene institute, a room for nurses, a room for female SS personnel, and finally a washroom and toilets. Upstairs lived 500 to 700 women prisoners, assigned to be the subjects of the experiments conducted in block no. 10. Also there was located Weber's so-called "*Bluttspendung*," where blood was collected from the women and then sent in ampoules to the hygiene institute in Rajsko. Prof. Clauberg and the Hauptsturmführer, a gynecologist, Dr. Wirths, carried out the experiments in block no. 10. Clauberg continued the experiments that he had begun in block no. 30 in Birkenau. He came to Auschwitz from time to time and, on each occasion, carried out several experiments the same way he had in block no. 30; that is, he gave the women injections to the inside of their reproductive parts, and then took x-rays in the x-ray room and photographed them. Clauberg's assistant, a chemist named Dr. Gebel [Johannes Goebel or Göbel – I.S.] accompanied him in February or perhaps March 1944. He was an SS man with a high officer's rank, but he wore civilian clothing. He set up a chemical laboratory for himself in block no. 10, in which he made creams, toothpaste, and other cosmetic articles. Additionally, he worked in that laboratory on developing his own substitute that would cause the temporary sterilization of women. In connection with this, he performed procedures on women in the same way as Clauberg. In Gebel's time, these procedures took place on a mass scale. He performed an average of 30 of these procedures a day, and sometimes even 75 in a single day. This state of affairs lasted until the end of the camp's existence. Aside from Gebel, Clauberg himself continued to carry out procedures sporadically, driving to the camp for that purpose and also conferring frequently with Gebel. According to my calculations, Clauberg and Gebel together carried out these procedures on about 1,000 women. (...)

After coming to block no. 10, I was assigned to the experimental station belonging to Dr. Wirths. However, I was also able to go into Clauberg's station and observe what went on there. As a nurse, I was seconded on more than one occasion from Wirths's station to Clauberg's, and saw with my own eyes the course of the procedures performed by Clauberg or Gebel. (...) The experimental work by Clauberg and Gebel was a secret, and none of the prisoner doctors was admitted to the experimental station, or took part in the procedures performed there. On the other hand, the Auschwitz camp commandants Rudolf Höss, Schwarz, Ber [Baer – I.S.], and other high SS dignitaries visited Clauberg's experimental station on more than one occasion, were present in the course of the procedures, and took a lively interest in the work of Clauberg and Gebel. Clauberg and Gebel performed their experiments on women not only for the purpose of finding a substance that would induce sterility in women. They were also interested in trying out various substitute preparations that could be used as contrast material in X-rays of the female reproductive organs. Whether and to what degree their efforts in this direction were successful, I am unable to say.

Source: APMA-B, Höss Trial Collection, vol. 7, pp. 74–78.

Excerpt from testimony at the trial of Rudolf Höss by Alina Białosto-cka [at camp under the name Brewda], former prisoner no. 62761, employed at experimental block no. 10 in the main camp, where, as a gynecologist-surgeon, she held the post of chief block doctor with the rights of block supervisor for a time.

Professor Clauberg's experiments consisted of injecting contrast material (Lipiodol and Iodipine) into the uterus and Fallopian tubes, and taking x-ray photographs of the reproductive organs. This procedure was carried out brutally, and often caused complications in the form of peritonitis, inflammation of the ovaries, and high fever. (…)

No one, not even female SS personnel, was allowed into the room where the experiments took place. I was present three times during the experiments. The first time, Dr. Clauberg himself called me in because a patient had collapsed on the table and I, as a doctor, was supposed to save her. The second and third times were during experiments carried out by Goebel, who had two patients collapse one after the other on the table. I saved all of them, but as a result of the experiments they came down with peritonitis and inflammation of the uterine appendages (3–4 months).

Source: APMA-B, Höss Trial Collection, vol. 17, pp. 59–80.

Testimony by former prisoner Mitie Harpman, a Dutch Jew born in Amsterdam in 1902, who was a victim of experiments in block no. 10 in the Auschwitz Main Camp. She gave this deposition to the Soviet Commission at the site of the Auschwitz camp in February 1945.

In March 1944,[11] Professor Clauberg came to Auschwitz and resumed performing experiments on me in April; namely, I was laid down naked on a black table, and covered from above with a clear, illuminated pane. The lights in the operating room were turned off. Next, some sort of device was placed in my vagina. I felt pain like that of childbirth. A red light came on. Then they took pictures. Professor Clauberg himself conducted this experiment, and there was one other German doctor with him–I do not know his name. They took a picture the next day, but did not place the device in my vagina. Next, this same experiment was repeated two weeks later, and again two weeks after that. Aside from these experiments, in the meantime, I was given some sort of injections in my breasts, 3 injections the first time and a further 9 injections all at once several days later. The German doctors Gubels (Goebel) and Weber carried out this experiment with the injections. In July 1944, Professor Clauberg came a second time and, saying that I was no longer useful for the experiments, sent me to Birkenau. They sent 12 other women there with me. The rest remained in block no. 10. While I was in the experimental hospital in block no. 10, I heard from other women that Professor Clauberg himself had told them that he had bought 300 women from the commandant for experiments and that, after the appropriate experiments in Auschwitz, he would send them to Germany.

Source: APMA-B, Statements Collection, vol. 1, p. 47.

---

[11] Clauberg began his sterilization experiments at the end of 1942.

Excerpt from an account by Apolonia Tusznio, former prisoner number 63873, victim of criminal sterilization experiments.

Block no. 10 was the experimental block. (…) Gynecological experiments on Jewish women prisoners were conducted there. A German doctor by the name of Clauberg carried out these experiments.

Although I was an Aryan, I also was designated for experimental purposes. The reason for this is that I, too, was sentenced to death.

I spent 3 months in block no. 10. Only in the third month of my stay in block no. 10 did Dr. Clauberg operate on me. Before the operation, several procedures were conducted on me consisting of injections to the vagina. I do not know what these injections were. They were very painful. After the injection I had powerful chills that lasted for 12 hours.

After two weeks spent in bed after the operation, an ambulance took me to the women's camp in Birkenau. I was placed in block no. 22 and assigned to labor in the penal labor detail designated as no. 21. The labor in penal labor detail no. 21 consisted of draining the fields, harvesting grain in Rajsko, digging in the earth, and plowing. (…)

After the operation, I was very weak. I felt bad and kept crying, because I realized that I was permanently harmed for the rest of my life. (…)

The experiments carried out on me in block no. 10 left me infertile.

Source: APMA-B, Statements Collection, vol. 27, p. 31.

Horst Schumann

Medical doctor, member of the NSDAP, Luftwaffe lieutenant, SS-Sturmbannführer. Born May 1, 1906 in Halle. From August 1939 director of the euthanasia center at Grafeneck in Wurttemburg, then of the Sonnenstein euthanasia center (near Pirna) from December 1940. First came to Auschwitz in July 1941 to select chronically ill and disabled prisoners for the 14f13 program (a continuation of the T-4 program for the killing of the ill and disabled). During this first Auschwitz selection, he sentenced 575 prisoners to death (under the pretext of a stay at a sanatorium in Dresden). They were killed with carbon dioxide in the showers of the Sonnenstein euthanasia center. Schumann returned to Auschwitz in late 1942 to work out a cheap and quick sterilization method. He carried out experiments in sterilization by x-ray on several hundred male and female Jewish prisoners. After the war, he lived in West Germany until 1951. A trial of those who carried out the euthanasia program was held in June and July 1947 in Tübingen, but he was not arrested.

In 1955 he settled in Sudan, from where he fled to Nigeria in 1959. In 1960 he was living in Ghana and practicing medicine at the Health Ministry. Under the pressure of world public opinion he was arrested in 1966 and extradited to West Germany. He was arraigned before a jury in Frankfurt am Main on September 23 and indicted for crimes connected with euthanasia. The crimes he had committed in Auschwitz were to be included in a separate indictment. The charges against him were dismissed on grounds of ill health in April 1971.

Horst Schumann. The photograph at right was provided by the International Auschwitz Committee, December 1966. (APMA-B, neg. no. 423).

DOC.NO. 205

XIa/126

Der Reichsfuehrer SS
1314/4

11. August 1942

SS-Oberfuehrer Brack
Berlin W 8
Vosstr. 4

Feld/Kommandostelle

G e h e i m e R e i c h s s a c h e

4 Ausfertigungen
4. Ausfertigung

1.) Lieber B r a c k

Ich komme erst heute dazu, Ihnen den Empfang Ihres
Briefes vom 23.6. zu bestaetigen. Ich habe ein Absolutes
Interesse, dass die Sterilisierung durch Roentgenstrahlen
mindestens in einem Lager einmal in einer Versuchsreihe
erprobt wird. Ich waere Reichsleiter Bouhler sehr dank
bar, wenn er die sachverstaendigen Aerzte zunaechst einmal
fuer die Versuchsreihe zur Verfuegung stellen wuerde.

Der Reichsarzt SS sowie der zustaendige Hauptamtschef fuer
die Konzentrationslager erhalten von mir einen Durchschlag
dieses Briefes.

Heil Hitler
Ihr
gez. H. Himmler

2.) SS-Obergruppenfuehrer P o h l

3.) SS-Gruppenfuehrer Dr. G r a w i t z

mit der Bitte um Kenntnisnahme

I.A.

SS-Obersturmfuehrer

11. August 1942

A CERTIFIED TRUE COPY

- 1 -

Letter from the Reichsführer SS to SS-Oberführer Victor Brack of Hitler's chancellery, in which he states that he is interested in sterilization by x-rays in the concentration camps. (APMA-B, neg. no. 441).

Translation:

DOC. No. 206
XIa/126

Reichsführer SSAugust 11, 1942
1314/4

SS-Oberführer Brack   Field Headquarters
Berlin V 8
Vosstr. 4

<u>Secret State Business</u>

   1.)   Dear Brack,
   Only today am I able to confirm the receipt of your letter of June 23. I am interested to the highest degree in sterilization by x-rays being tested at least once in a camp in a series of experiments. I would be extremely grateful to Reichsleiter <u>Bouhler</u> [head of Hitler's chancellery] if he would above all make expert doctors available to carry out the series of experiments.

   The SS-Reicharzt [head physician of the SS] and the relevant head of the main office [economic and administrative] for concentration camps are receiving copies of this letter from me.

   Heil Hitler
   (signature)
   Yours
   H. Himmler

   <u>2.)   SS-Obergruppenführer P o h l</u>
   <u>3.)   SS-Gruppenführer D r. G r a w i t z</u>

Return contact requested

Authorized.
SS-Obersturmführer

November 11, 1942

A CERTIFIED TRUE COPY

Geheime Reichssache

Berlin W8, den 29. April 1944
Voßstraße 4
Fernruf: Ortsverkehr 12 00 54
Fernverkehr 12 66 21

Kanzlei des Führers
der NSDAP.

Aktenzeichen: IIa/Kt.

An den
Reichsführer-SS. und Chef der
Deutschen Polizei
Heinrich H i m m l e r

B e r l i n SW 11
Prinz Albrecht Str. 9

Sehr verehrter Reichsführer!

Im Auftrage von Reichsleiter Bouhler überreiche ich
Ihnen anliegend eine Arbeit des Dr. Horst S c h u -
m a n n über die Einwirkung der Röntgenstrahlen auf
die menschlichen Keimdrüsen.

Sie baten seinerzeit Oberführer Brack um Durchführung
dieser Arbeit und unterstützten dieselbe durch Zurver-
fügungstellung des entsprechenden Materials im KL.
Auschwitz. Ich verweise speziell auf den 2. Teil der
vorliegenden Arbeit, der den Nachweis führt, daß eine
Kastration des Mannes auf diesem Wege ziemlich ausge-
schlossen ist oder einen Aufwand erfordert, der sich
nicht lohnt. Die operative Kastration, die, wie ich
mich selbst überzeugt habe, nur 6 - 7 Minuten dauert,
ist demnach zuverlässiger und schneller zu bewerkstelli-
gen als die Kastration mit Röntgenstrahlen.

Eine Fortsetzung der Arbeit werde ich Ihnen demnächst
überreichen können.

Heil Hitler!

Anlage.

Letter from deputy head of the 2nd department of the Führer chancellery, Blankenburg, reporting to the Reichsführer SS on Dr. Schumann's experiments in Auschwitz. (APMA-B, neg. no. 132/2).

Translation:

Berlin, April 29, 1944

Chancellery of the Führer
NSDAP

Secret State Business!

To
Reichsführer SS and Commander
of the German Police
Heinrich H i m m l e r

Registry no: IIa/Kt.

B e r l i n SW 11
Prinz-Albrecht Str. 9

Most Esteemed Reichsführer!

On the recommendation of Reich Chancellery Director Bouhler, I am enclosing a work by Dr. Horst Schumann on the effects of x-rays on the human reproductive glands.

At some point, you have asked Herr Oberführer Brack for permission to carry out this work and for support in the form of the appropriate material being placed at his disposal in Auschwitz concentration camp. I draw your attention to the second part of the work submitted to you, in which evidence is provided that the castration of men in the proposed way is rather to be ruled out, or requires efforts that are not worth making. Surgical castration, which–as I myself have learned–takes only 6–7 minutes, is far more reliable in the light of the results obtained, and quicker to perform than castration with the use of x-rays.

I will be able to send you the next part of this work in the nearest future.

Heil Hitler!
(illegible signature)

Enclosure.
1940/44 (rest illegible)

318

Lfd. Nr.	Datum	Häftl. Nr.	Name u. Vorname	D-i-a-g-n-o-s-e
19.510	10.11.	125948	Freund Frans Isr.	Phlegm. reg. genu sin.
1	"	41579 FL	Malali Eleonora	Casus explorationis
2	"	46614 FL	Warsano Dora	–"– –"–
3	"	38968 FL	Azi Rigeta	–"– –"–
4	"	40574 FL	Beracha Lissie	–"– –"–
5	"	38782 FL	Kohen Dora	–"– –"–
6	"	13339 FL	Mordo Rachel	–"– –"–
7	"	41317 FL	Bihau Buena	–"– –"–
8	"	38762 FL	Biwas Flora	–"– –"–
9	"	40204 FL	Gilda Thermin	–"– –"–
19.520	"	41452 FL	Mellach Bella	–"– –"–
1	"	62378	Makowski Janusz	Otitis med. purul. meso et retrotymp. sin.
2	11.11.	159601	Dziatosynistie Sender	Panar. dig. IV manus dex.
3	"	157317	Fuchs Stephan	Ulcus cruris dex.
4	"	152386	Saracyn Georg	Furunc. –"– –"–
5	"	11335	Rabster Daniel	Bulla abc. dig. III manus dex.
6	"	55789	Arest Juri	Absc. reg. tempor. sin.
7	"	120319	Kozara Joseph	–"– axillae dex.
8	"	48524	Apfelbaum Sichon	Panar. pollicis manus sin.
9	"	136275	Hohonienko Peter	Paron. dig. III manus sin.
19.530	"	144176	Lyhanok Iwan	Furunc. capitis
1	"	131084	Rosenberg Herman	Furunc. palpebrae dex.
2	"	99494	Lidemieki Lazar	Panar. dig. III manus dex.
3	"	154821	Laska Michael	Absc. reg. auriculi sin.
4	"	159861	Draganow Alex.	Furunc. nuchae
5	"	1470 FL	Guthmann Lotti	Appendicitis chronica
6	"	106658	Freuher Harry Isr.	Hernia inguin. dex.
7	"	142092	Lubka Abram	Mucosae ani
8	"	157156	Messerschmidt Isser	Varices haemorrhoidales
9	"	180643	Dresden Samuel	Phlegm. necrotic. antibrachii sin.
19.540	"	55829	Fedorowicz Wasyl	–"– –"– –"– dex.
1	"	106313	Abdinar Andreas	Absc. antibrachii sin.
2	"	141369	Malinowski Leib	Tumor scroti
3	"	61883	Klimek Johann	Rhinitis hypertrophica

A page from the surgical records book in block no. 21 (surgical) of the Auschwitz I camp hospital. It includes the name of Dora Akunis (in Auschwitz under the name Cohen), camp no. 38782, and the names of 9 of her fellow prisoners subjected to x-ray sterilization experiments. (Dora Akunis's account is included in this selection of documents and materials). (APMA-B, micr. no. 115/318–319).

```
H.-Krankenbau des                          Auschwitz, den 16. Dezember 1943.
K. L. Auschwitz I
```

103

Tätigkeitsbericht der chirurgischen Abteilung
des H.-Krankenbaues des K.L.Auschwitz I., für
die Zeit vom 16.9.1943 bis 15.12.1943.

Die chirurgische Abteilung war während des Berichts-
vierteljahres, wie vordem, in Block 21 untergebracht.
Wegen Raummangel im Block 21 wurde jedoch ein Teil
der zahlreichen chirurgischen Fälle auf der chirurgischen Abteilung des Blockes 19 behandelt. Ambulante
chirurgische Behandlungen haben in der Ambulanz des
Häftl.-Krankenbaues, im Block 28, stattgefunden.

In der Berichtszeit wurden auf allen Abteilungen der
chirurgischen Station insgesamt 1800 Häftlinge behandelt. Bei diesen wurden 314 grössere aseptische Operationen durchgeführt. Die Zahl der septischen Eingriffe (bei Phlegmonen, Abzesse usw.) beträgt 2135 Fälle.

Von den aseptischen Operationen sind zu erwähnen:

  2 Resektiones ventriculi
  3 Strumectomien
  1 Cholecystectomie
  2 Laparatomien bei perforiertem ulcus ventriculi,
    bei peritonitis etc.
 10 Appendicektomien
102 Herniotomien
 89 Testisamputationen
  1 Kastration
  5 Sterilisationen
  9 Hydrocoelen
  7 Varicotomien nach Langenbeck
  2 Varicotomien nach Babcock
  3 Haluces valgi
 11 Gliedmassen-Amputationen
 30 Antrotomien
 30 Tonsillectomien
 16 Conchotomien
 10 Ovariotomien
  1 Resektion capitis humari
  1 Salpingectomie
  1 Colpo-perineoplastik
  2 Thoracoplastiken
  1 Debrudement

Nebstdem wurden einige kleinere septischen Eingriffe ge-
macht, wie tenolysis, ~~anudestis, lyponatia~~ u.dgl.
Von den übrigen septischen Behandlungen bei Phlegmonen,
Vereiterungen usw., entfallen auf

    untere Extremitäten   997 Eingriffe
    obere Extremitäten   555   "
    bei verschiedenen
    chirurgischen Er-
    krankungen   583   "

**Report by the director of the surgical department of the prisoner
hospital in Auschwitz I for the period from September 16 to December 15, 1943, in which he reports that castration was carried out 106
times in the camp hospital (*Hodenamputationen, Genitalienopera-
tionen, Eierstockentfernung, Entfernung des Eileiters*).**
(APMA-B, D. Au II – 5/1, p. 103–104).

104

- 2 -

Die Heilungstendenz der postoperativen, aseptischen
Wunden ist 95 v.H. per primam, 5 v.H. per secundam.
Die Sterblichkeit beträgt im allgemeinen auf allen
Abteilungen 56 Fälle, d.i. 3.01 v.H. der Gesamtzahl
der behandelten Patienten.

Die aseptischen Eingriffe wurden gewöhnlich mit Aether-
Narkose oder mit 2%-Novocain-Betäubung ausgeführt. Bei
der kleinen, septischen Wundversorgung wurde gewöhnlich Chloräthyl-Lösung verwendet. In der Berichtszeit
machte sich ein Mangel an narkotischen Mitteln für
kurz andauernde Narkosen (Chloräthyl) empfindlich be-
merkbar.

Das Fehlen eines Wundversorgungsraumes in der aseptischen
Abteilung wirkt sich sehr nachteilig für die Behand-
lung der postoperativen Fälle aus und erschwert ihre
Heilung.

Die Operationswäsche befindet sich, infolge ständigen
Gebrauches und wegen Mangel an Austauschmöglichkeiten,
in sehr schlechtem Zustand.

                              Der Lagerarzt des
                              K. L. Auschwitz I

                              SS-Obersturmführer.

Second page of the report by the head of the surgical department.

Translation:

Prisoner Hospital   Auschwitz, December 16, 1943
Auschwitz I Concentration Camp

Report on the work of the surgical department of the prisoner hospital in Auschwitz I Concentration Camp for the period from 16.9.1943 to 15.12.1943

In the quarter covered by this report, as indicated above, the surgical department was located in block no. 21. Because of the overcrowding in block no. 21, some of the numerous surgical cases were nevertheless operated on in the surgical department in block no. 19. Outpatient surgical procedures were carried out in the outpatient clinic of the prisoner hospital in block no. 28.

During the period covered by the report a total of 1,800 prisoners underwent surgical procedures in all the surgical departments. They included 314 aseptic operations. The number of septic operations (cases of suppuration, pustules, etc.) was 2,135.

Among the aseptic operations, the following should be mentioned:

2 gastrectomy (Magenresektion)
3 strumectomies (removal of the thyroid gland)
1 cholecystectomies (removal of the gallbladder)
2 laparotomies of perforated stomach ulcers (ulcus ventriculi) with peritonitis, etc.
10 removals of the appendix (appendectomy)
102 operations on groin hernias (herniotomia)
89 testicular amputations (testis amputationa)
1 castration
5 sterilizations
9 removals of hydroceles
7 ovarectomies by Langenbeck's method
2 ovarectomies by Babcock's method
3 removals of bunions (haluces valgi)
11 limb amputations
30 anthrotomies
30 tonsillectomies
16 conchotomies (incisions of nasal conchae)
10 ovariotomies (removal of the ovaries)
1 resection of the capitis humani
1 salpingectomy (removal of the Fallopian tubes)
1 colpoperineoplastica (plastic surgery of the vagina and crotch)

2 thoracoplasticas (reshaping the thorax through removal of the ribs)
1 debridement (surgical wound cleaning and removal of dead tissue)

Aside from this, there were also several more minor septic procedures carried out, such as tenolysis (freeing a tendon from adhesions), etc.

The remaining septic procedures involving phlegmons, suppuration, etc. can be divided thus:

Lower extremities	997 procedures
Upper extremities	555 procedures
Surgery in various	
Other cases	583 procedures

The tendency for the healing of postoperative aseptic wounds is 95% *per primam*, 5% *per secundam*. The overall death rate in all departments is 56 cases, that is 3.01 v. H. of the total number of patients treated.

Aseptic procedures were carried out with the use of narcosis with ether or anesthesia with 2% Novocain. Chlorethyl solution was used to dress smaller, septic incisions. During the period covered by the report, the lack of narcotic means for brief narcosis (chlorethyl) became all too apparent.

The lack of a room for dressing wounds in the aseptic department had a very unfavorable impact on the treatment of post-operative cases, and impaired recovery.

The operating garments, as a result of their constant use and in view of the lack of any way to change them—are in poor condition.

Camp Physician
Auschwitz I Concentration Camp

(illegible signature)
SS-Obersturmführer

Excerpt of an explanation given to the Supreme National Tribunal in Poland by former Auschwitz commandant SS-Obersturmbannführer Rudolf Höss (1947) on Nazi doctor Horst Schumann's sterilization experiments.

On orders from Hitler's chancellery (*Kanzlei des Führers*), air force Ober-leutnant Dr. Schumann experimented on inducing artificial infertility with the use of x-rays.

Schumann came to Auschwitz for the second time in 1942, when the women's camp had already been transferred from Auschwitz to Birkenau. His arrival was preceded by an order from Himmler, according to which Schumann was coming to Auschwitz in order to conduct sterilization ex-periments on female Jewish prisoners using x-rays. According to this order, I was supposed to put the number of prisoners Schumann required at his disposal and give him all necessary help. After Schumann's arrival and the installation of his apparatus in one of the blocks in the women's camp in Birkenau (block no. 28, sector BIa),[12] he began carrying out his procedures on women on a mass scale. (…)

I personally observed the Schumann procedures and saw that he ex-posed women to x-rays from the front, side, and back in the region of their reproductive organs. I understood from the way these procedures were carried out and from talking to Schumann that he was not follow-ing any scientific principles and was simply trying to find a solution to the problem that had been posed for him, which was not, in any case, of any particular personal interest to him. When I asked him how he intended to measure the results of his procedures or establish norms for their practical application in the future, he was either unwilling or unable to give me any satisfactory answer. (…)

In the initial stage, the women exposed to radiation by Schumann were placed in the camp hospital. At a later time, the majority of them went to the residential blocks and to work. The majority of the women exposed to Schumann's procedures died. (…) From discussions with garrison physi-cian Wirths, I know that, after Schumann's x-rays, the women suffered the destruction (*Zerstörung*) of their organisms. (…)

I could not provide any figures on the number of women subjected to Schumann's procedures, but in any case it was in the hundreds. Schumann carried out all his experimentation on Jewish women, and he knew that they were sentenced to die in the camp. Schumann himself was interested neither in the outcome of his experiments nor in the fate of his patients. I know of no case in which he gave any of them medical treatment. At a later time, Schumann received permission from Himmler to carry out his procedures on men.

Source: APMA-B, Höss Trial Collection, vol. 21, pp. 137–139.

---

[12] In fact, barrack no. 30 in the women's camp in Birkenau (sector BIa).

Excerpt from an account submitted during the Höss Trial by Michał Kula, former prisoner number 2718, a member of the locksmiths' labor detail, of Dr. Horst Schumann's sterilization experiments.

In the fall of 1942, a Wehrmacht flier, Oberleutnant, Obermedizinal-Rat, Dr. Schumann, a professor from Berlin, appeared in Auschwitz. He was a man of about 38, blond, tall, with a dueling scar on his left cheek. With the help of Siemens engineers and employees, he installed two x-ray machines in block no. 30 of the Birkenau women's camp. After the Siemens employees left, Schumann entrusted a Czech, Stanisław Slezak,[13] employed in the Bauleitung electricians' detail, to maintain the machines. I lived in the same block as Slezak. He told me what the machines were used for and how they were built. The x-ray machines were mounted on metal frames and moved on rails set in concrete. Each device contained an x-ray source. They were rated at 250 thousand volts and 40 milliamperes. The power cables were constructed in such a way as to be cooled by oil flowing inside the cables. In the reservoirs of the pumps was a copper coil through which cold water was pumped to cool the oil and the mercury fuse that protected the machine from overheating. Both machines were connected by cables to a cabin with double walls shielded by 5 mm. of lead. The control panel for the x-ray machines was inside. Schumann sat inside this cabin, which had leaded windows, observing the procedures and controlling the x-ray dosage. These machines were used to sterilize women and men. The women were seated on a stool between the two machines, with one x-ray tube in the area of their back, and the other one at the front. The exposure was 5 to 15 minutes. Schumann himself regulated the voltage and intensity of the current and the time of exposure, depending on what he intended to accomplish through the exposure. After the procedure, many women vomited then and there. We saw them returning on foot from Birkenau to Auschwitz, where they were housed in block no. 10. They walked hunched over, holding their bellies.

Many of the women in block no. 10 died from burns to the parts of their bodies that were irradiated. Others, who developed abscesses, were sent to the gas or jabbed [given lethal injections of phenol to the heart]. Men were irradiated with a single machine. Only one testicle was burned, while the other was shielded with lead during irradiation. After the procedure, they returned to normal blocks and had one day off at most. The next day, regardless of their state of health, they were forced to work. Many of the men died as a result of the radiation. Some of those who survived were castrated by Schumann in the hospital a month later. Schumann kept their testicles

---

[13] Stanislav Slezak, a Czech prisoner, camp number 39340, sent to Mauthausen on January 5, 1945 as a "*Geheimnisträger*" (bearer of secrets); shot in the crematorium there on April 3.

in jars and took them to Berlin. He chose mainly young, healthy people for his procedures, mostly Jewish men and women from Greece, who were chosen by Schillinger[14] from particular blocks at Schumann's request. In a single session, Schumann carried out procedures on approximately 30 women. (…)

Schumann also used the apparatus described here in experiments on the treatment of cancer. For this purpose, he was supplied with Gypsy children age 3 to 16. These children were chosen in the Gypsy camp. They had cancerous abscesses on their heads, usually in their mouths or on their lips. We were told that these were induced through artificial grafts. Schumann conducted these experiments on approximately 80 Gypsy children, all of whom died. These people were placed at the exclusive disposal of Schumann, who went to the Gypsy camp and chose children for experimentation.

Source: APMA-B, Höss Trial Collection, vol. 2, pp. 81–83.

---

[14] SS-Oberscharführer Josef Schillinger, *Rapportführer* in the Birkenau men's camp (sector BIId). Shot dead on October 23, 1943 by a Jewish women deported to Auschwitz in a transport of 1,800 people from Bergen-Belsen.

Excerpt from a deposition submitted to the Soviet Commission on the grounds of the liberated camp in February 1945 by former prisoner Jakow Skurnik, a Polish Jewish victim of Dr. Horst Schumann's experiments.

I do not remember the exact date in December 1942 when the block supervisor in my block announced that men between the ages of 18 and 30 would not go to work the following day, but go instead for mandatory x-rays according to a list to be made up. The day after this announcement, a list of men aged 18–30 was drawn up and all were sent to the women's camp, to block no. 31 [in fact, 30 – I.S.], where there were two x-ray machines that the Germans called special x-ray machines. Between 55 and 60 men were sent to block no. 31, and they all went without fear because the block scribe explained that it would be warm in the x-ray office. For me, the most important thing was not that it would be warm, but rather that not going to work guaranteed me at least one more day of life–since, as I have mentioned earlier, between 50 and 60 people were killed at work each day. On the day when the group of 60 men was led to block no. 31, they began taking us two at a time through the x-ray machines. Before that, the men stripped naked. A horizontal board was attached to the x-ray machine, which came up to the level of the sex organs. The scrotum had to be placed on the board, and then a large electric lamp irradiated the scrotum, while the one being irradiated stood with his hands resting on his hips, at the back.

The irradiation of one man lasted 5 to 7 minutes. I did not feel any pain during the irradiation.

After we had all been irradiated or, as the doctors called it, after sterilization, we were sent to our previous jobs.

I do not know who carried out the sterilization, I do not know their names. They were dressed in decent civilian clothing. I assume that they were doctors.

Among the 60 people subjected to sterilization with me were friends of mine. (…)

Eight months after the sterilization, everyone who had it done was sent to the Auschwitz branch, to block no. 28, the Auschwitz [main camp – I.S.] hospital, where each one was individually questioned by a German doctor with the rank of captain (I do not know his name), dressed in a flyer's uniform. During the questioning, the captain asked if I had frequent erections, if I had nocturnal emissions, and a range of other questions the substance of which I do not recall. Afterwards, the captain who had questioned me carried out an experiment on me, forcing me to undertake an action with the purpose of stimulation. Then a metal pipe resembling a rod was introduced into my anus, a massage was performed, and sperm was gathered from my sexual organ, which the captain placed on a glass slide and examined under a microscope, making some sort of notes.

After the questioning and the experiment, I was directed along with the others to the surgical ward of the hospital in block no. 21, where each was hospitalized in room no. 4 to await some sort of operation, although I did not then specifically know what kind.

After two days, my friend Szlemowicz and I were taken into the operating room, where there were two doctors–the German [actually, Pole – I.S.] Dering and the Pole Grabczyński. I was laid on one table and Szlemowicz on the other. They gave me a shot in the hip and began carrying out the operation. After the injection, I could not feel exactly what the doctor was doing to me, but I saw that they removed my left testicle. Doctor Dering operated on (castrated) me and Grabczyński [operated on] Szmelowicz. That day, the whole group, 8 men, had their left testicles removed, and all were later hospitalized in room no. 4 and the wound from the operation was treated for 14 days. After recovery, I was discharged to the camp and assigned to labor at the bricklayers' school in block no. 7a. 6 months after the first operation, all of us had another one, that is, the second testicle was removed. Doctor Grabczyński performed the second operation on me.

I do not know how many men, aside from these eight, had the second operation. After the second operation, each was hospitalized for 2 weeks, and then sent to their place of work. I do not know to what ends the German fascists castrated me and the others. Sterilization and castration were conducted on prisoners of all nationalities, from various countries, but especially Greek Jews from Salonika. After the castration, all the capos harassed those who had been castrated, swearing at them in front of all the prisoners.

Source: APMA-B, Other Collections, 1/1, vol. 2, pp. 68–74.

Excerpt from an account by Józef (Dawid) Szarbel, former prisoner number 83397. He was castrated in July 1943.

Before morning roll call in July 1943, a commission made up of several SS men came to block no. 23A. They ordered the prisoners to line up in the corridor. During the inspection, the SS men chose several from among the hundred young, well built, healthy-looking Jews. I was one of those chosen. They led us out of the building and lined us up two-by-two. I was convinced they were going to lead us to block no. 11 and shoot us. Instead, they took us to hospital block no. 28. There were 16 or 18 of us–today I can no longer recall precisely.

In the corridor on the ground floor of block no. 28, they again lined us up two-by-two. There were many more prisoners there, all of them Jews. Here, we went through a new selection. Accompanied by other SS men and prisoner physicians, an SS physician sent some of the Jews to a room on the left side of the corridor, and others to a room on the right. They sent me to the left.

They ordered me to undress. They cuffed my wrists and ankles, and placed some kind of protective belt or loincloth on my belly. Then they placed me on an operating gurney and took me into the operating room.

There were several SS men in the operating room, some of them in white smocks and others not; a prisoner-physician, Dr. Dering, was also there. One of the SS men came up to me. I saw that he was wearing rubber gloves. He artificially brought me to the ejaculation of sperm. (…) Having obtained my sperm, they examined it under a microscope.

After a local anesthetic, Dr. Dering performed a surgical procedure on me, removing one of my testicles. I could see the operation in the mirror of the operating lamp. The SS men in attendance chatted during the procedure, jesting liberally. (…)

The removed testicle was thrown into a jar containing a bluish or greenish fluid. That jar already contained a dozen or more testicles removed from those who had gone before me.

They closed the wound with two clamps. After removing the cuffs from my wrists and ankles, they moved me to another room. Later, those who had been operated on were taken to hospital block no. 21, and I learned there that those sent to the room on the right side of the corridor of block no. 28 had been sentenced to even worse injuries. Both their testicles were cut off.

I remained in block no. 28 until the wound healed, that is, about four weeks. Next, I was sent to work in the *Neue Wäscherei* labor detail, and several days later transferred [to the sub-camp in Libiąż]. I do not know who arranged it, but perhaps the transfer to labor in the sub-camp protected me from further experimentation by the SS doctors.

Source: APMA-B, Statements Collection, vol. 46, pp. 31–32.

Excerpt from the memoirs of Dr. Rudolf Diem, former prisoner number 10022, employed in the outpatient clinic in block no. 28 in the main camp, on the subject of sterilization procedures.

In block no. 28 I saw men with extensive burns in the area of the lower belly and groin in a state of inflamed swollen skin resulting from x-rays. (…) I learned in block no. 21 about the subsequent fate of the irradiated men, who were castrated in the operating room in order to learn what changes were caused by the X-rays. I saw many of these post-operative cases some time later in the corpse room in block no. 28. If any of them lived, it was probably only because the prisoner doctors destroyed their medical records, erasing all trace of them.

Source: APMA-B, Memoirs Collection, vol. 172, pp. 134–135.

Excerpt from an account by Franciszek Gulba, former prisoner number 10245, on the subject of prisoners subjected to sterilization.

I went back to road building in camp BIb. The very next day, a group of 7 to 8t young prisoners were assigned to that labor detail; however, they walked hunched over, clutched at their lower abdomens, moaned, rolled around on the ground, and squirmed in pain. They spoke neither Polish nor German. I took the trouble of going to their block and discovered that they were 15- to 17-year-old Greek Jews on whom experiments of some kind had been performed. More such groups were sent on the next two days. It seems to me that it was the next day when I was called to the camp chancery, where Rapportführer Schilinger handed me a piece of paper bearing the numbers of the seven young prisoners (they were standing outside the office) in order to lead them to block no. 30 of the adjacent women's camp. A capo came out to meet me there, and he told me everything, that it was Dr. Schumann who was doing sterilization with an x-ray machine.

Source: APMA-B, Statements Collection vol. 70, pp. 57 b, c.

Excerpt from a deposition by Dr. Albert Flechner (a Jew from France), former prisoner number 65566, on the condition of prisoners subjected to sterilization. Deposed by the Soviet Commission at the site of the Auschwitz camp in February 1945.

When I was working as an orderly in the hospital, more or less in September 1943, about 30 post-operative men, all of whom had their testicles removed, were admitted to us, to block no. 9. Some had one testicle removed, and some both. They were all in serious condition. The operations were performed by a German doctor, Oberscharführer Entress, and a prisoner doctor, the Pole Dering. He (the Pole) was later released and went to work in Germany.[15] I do not remember the names of the sufferers whose testicles had been removed. Some of them died, and some of them were sent alive to the crematorium as a result of selections.

Translation from Russian into Polish by Alicja Wójcik.

Source: APMA-B, Soviet Commission Records IZ 1/1, vol. 2, p. 94.

---

[15]   Actually, he was employed in Clauberg's private clinic.

Excerpt from a deposition by Dr. Adolf Mec, a German Jew, former prisoner number B-13877, on the condition of prisoners subjected to sterilization. Deposed by the Soviet Commission at the site of the Auschwitz camp in February 1945.

We arrived at the Auschwitz camp on October 29, 1944. There were a total of 2,200 people in our transport. Our transport arrived from Germany. I was sent to Birkenau. I was given number B-13877. (…) While I was working in the camp hospital in Birkenau in November 1944, a patient with removed testicles was admitted, prisoner Grinwald whose first name I do not know. Grinwald had severe burns in the vicinity of his genitalia and an unhealed, suppurating wound where his testicles had been removed. Both his testicles had been removed. The burns and wound were so severe that patient Grinwald could not walk. He said that he had been subjected to sterilization at the beginning of 1943, that is x-rays had been administered, followed by the removal of his testicles. Grinwald underwent treatment with us until January 1945 and recovered to a small degree, and in January 1945, before the arrival of the Soviet troops, was sent in a transport of prisoners to Germany. Grinwald volunteered to leave with the transport because he feared being shot, which is why he declared himself healthy and joined the transport.

Translation from Russian into Polish by Alicja Wójcik.

Source: APMA-B, Soviet Commission Records IZ 1/1, vol. 2, p. 107.

Excerpt from a deposition by Dr. Maksym Grosman, a Jew from Yugoslavia, former prisoner number A-5419, who treated prisoners subjected to sterilization experiments. Deposed by the Soviet Commission at the site of the Auschwitz camp in February 1945.

I am not aware of cases of the sterilization of women. On the subject of men I know this much: how the castration was carried out and at exactly what time I do not know, but in 1944, from September to December, as a doctor I treated four men whose names I do not remember who had undergone removal of the testicles. These sufferers told me that at the beginning they had been subjected to sterilization by x-ray, as a result of which they received severe burns, but regardless of this their testicles were removed for research purposes after the sterilization. The Germans sent three of them to the crematorium, and in January 1945 they sent the one who had recovered to Germany in a transport of prisoners. I do not know which of the doctors carried out these experiments and operations.

Translation from Russian into Polish by Alicja Wójcik.

Source: APMA-B, Soviet Commission Records IZ 1/1, vol. 2, p. 98.

Excerpt from an account by Dr. Tadeusz Paczuła, former prisoner number 7725, employed in the hospital chancery in the main camp, on prisoners subjected to sterilization.

Horst Schumann came to Auschwitz on a permanent basis in November 1942. (…) Schumann chose young Jewish women. He sterilized them by placing the plates of the x-ray apparatus on the lower abdomens and buttocks of the victims. In this way he burned out their ovaries, also causing superficial burns and severe pain, with inflammation and peritoneal inflammation and adhesions. (…) After irradiation with x-rays the women returned to work, and were called in for operations two or three months later. The operations were performed very quickly, especially when they were done in block no. 21. These procedures were done with spinal anesthesia. Operations were also performed in block no. 10, where the cleanliness of the operating room left much to be desired. Patients died after the operations, with extensive wounds and suppurating pus from the extensive incisions. Their corpses were taken to the hospital morgue in block no. 28, and I saw them there quite often. They were always kept separately. The operations in block no. 10 were performed by Schumann with Dr. Samuel, and others supposedly assisted them. (…)

In most cases, the x-rays were administered in the Birkenau camp, while the hysterectomy was done in the main camp. Schumann carried out male experiments simultaneously. He chose his victims in the Birkenau camp and personally performed the irradiation of the male testicles. The irradiation differed–total or partial. With partial, a lead plate was used as a screen. Schumann irradiated about 30 people a day, performing these „procedures" two or three times a week. The irradiation varied from 5 to 15 minutes per male or female patient. In the men, such procedures resulted in extensive local or generalized inflammatory changes, changes and wounds resulting from burns, suppurating eczema of the skin, and inflammatory reactions in the direction of the peritoneum. Both men and women had violent reactions to the irradiation. Vomiting, nausea, painful spasms and serious complications, including fatal ones, were not rare. The women and men on whom Schumann carried out his experiments aged prematurely, and after the operations young girls looked elderly. After the operation, Schumann collected the „material" cut out of his victims for histopathological analysis. It should be added that the research victims went normally to work with their labor details and received no special consideration.

Schumann also took Jewish men he had chosen to the main camp and experimented with semen, obtaining it through masturbation, which took place in blocks nos. 19, 20, and 28. The bedraggled Jews walked from Birkenau to Auschwitz, still hungry from the previous day, only to have a handle stuck in their anuses in order to stimulate their glands in this way until the emission of semen. This procedure was highly painful and the production of sperm surely badly impaired, so that it usually took a very long time to achieve the intended effect. These prisoners begged for mercy, and after the procedure they returned hungry to Birkenau for evening roll call, only to learn that they had missed supper.

Schumann castrated male prisoners. Some of those who were castrated had been exposed to x-rays, and others not. The operations differed in degree. Biopsies were taken of one or both testicles, as well as the removal of one or both. (…)

These descriptions come from first-hand observation, conversations with the victims, and conversations with friends who were present when various kinds of things were done, either as auxiliaries or cleaners. I had official contact with block no. 10. Block no. 10 did not have its own chancery, and the HKB-Schreibstube often handled correspondence for block no. 10, and took delivery of correspondence, documentation, and materials such as x-ray photographs for block no. 10. (…) I often went inside block no. 10 and sent clerks who were friends of mine and under my command there on official business, and I had contacts with the prisoner functionaries in block no. 10 – with the block supervisor, her assistant (Rosa), the room supervisor Fanny (a Slovakian Jew), Sylwia Friedmann from the gynecologist's office, and Genia Lewin from the x-ray office, and also with prisoner doctors from the block no. 21 operating room–Dr. Dering, Dr. Grabczyński, Dr. Sobieszczański, Dr. Górecki, and Dr. Ławski. I was also on very good terms with the prisoner Władimir Złamał, who did color and monochromatic posters and drawings connected with the experimental work for Schumann.

Source: APMA-B, Statements Collection, vol. 53., pp. 205–208.

Excerpts from testimony at the trial of Rudolf Höss by Alina Biało-stocka [at camp under the name Brewda], former prisoner number 62761, employed at experimental block no. 10 in the main camp where, as a gynecologist-surgeon, she held the post of chief block doctor with the status of block supervisor for a time.

The SS doctor, Obersturmführer Schumann, who passed himself off as a professor even though there were SS men who had their doubts, used part of block no. 10 for experiments in the sterilization of men and women. His experimental station was located in Birkenau, and he sporadically used the x-ray room in block no. 10, where operations were carried out on his orders.

Experiments were made on young boys age 18 to 28 and girls from 15 to 19, to the number of about 60 women and about 700 men, 90% Greek Jews. As one stage in his procedure, Schumann irradiated the testicles of men and the vicinity of the ovaries in women with x-rays. He applied castration [sterilization] doses. On Schumann's orders, 4–6 weeks later, prisoner doctors removed the left ovary in one series and the right in the other series. The excised ovaries were sent to Hamburg for microscopic analysis. Those operated on frequently had peritonitis, inflammation of the uterus, with high fever and, often, internal hemorrhaging that led to death. The integument usually did not heal and suppurated copiously. After healing, there were symptoms of premature menopause: weight gain, hairiness, hot flushes, headaches, sweating spells, and psychological changes. The women patients suffered a great deal after the procedures, because the abdomen remained open. After these procedures, the patients were sent back to Birkenau or Auschwitz, from where most of them went to the gas chambers. (…) Operations for Dr. Schumann (…) were carried out by prisoner doctors: the previously mentioned Dr. Samuel, and Dr. Władysław Dering.

Source: APMA-B, Höss Trial Collection, vol. 17, pp. 59–80.

Excerpt from an account by Dora Akunis, former prisoner number 38782, a Greek Jew deported to Auschwitz from the Thessalonica ghetto on March 20, 1943 who became a victim of Dr. Schumann's experiments.

More or less in the middle of March 1943, I was deported along with other Jews from Thessalonica to Birkenau. (…) During a morning roll call in the summer of 1943, the block supervisor called out a certain number of girls, including me. (…) We were taken under guard to Auschwitz, to block no. 10. There were already other Greek women and girls there. Schumann came there one day–I learned his name while I was in block no. 10–and ordered all the girls to line up. He pointed to several girls, including me, and jotted down our numbers. The next day, they took us back to Birkenau and we were irradiated there. We went into a room and undressed, and were called from there one by one into another, dark room. There were two people there, Dr. Schumann and his assistant. The assistant placed two plates on my body, one on my belly and one on my back. Dr. Schumann went into a shielded cabin, observed me through the window, and turned on the apparatus that the plates were part of. I was standing inside the apparatus. It was turned on for several minutes; I do not know exactly how long. They took us back to Auschwitz that same day. We all vomited along the way. We did not know what had been done to us. Several days later, running sores appeared in the places where the plates had applied to us. (…) After about two months, they sent us back to work at Birkenau, even though our wounds had still not healed. (…) During morning roll call one day, they called out my number and the numbers of other girls who had been irradiated. They took us back to Auschwitz, to block no. 10. (…) Dr. Samuel examined us there (…) From among us, he chose Gilda and Bella for operations. Dr. Samuel operated on Gilda and Bella. As far as I recall, it was on the same day he examined them. (…) The operation took place in block no. 10, the same one we were staying in. (…) At some point in November 1943, they took me and 9 other girls to block no. 21, next door, and operated on us there (…) We had to undress in the antechamber to the operating room, and they gave us injections. (…) At the moment of receiving the injection, I lost all feeling in the lower part of my body. Some time later, they took me into the operating room and laid me on the table. Dr. Schumann and Dr. Dering were in that room, and another prisoner doctor, and a woman, Dr. Brewda. The latter kept my spirits up. There was a screen between the upper and lower parts of my body. I know that Dr. Dering operated on me, assisted by the second prisoner doctor. They took me back to block no. 10 after the operation. We were all lying in the same room, crying out in pain. (…) Later that night, Bella died. Beuna had a horrific open wound. Her wound, like ours, was running with pus. (…) After one or two months, Dr. Schumann appeared in the block. He looked at our wounds and ordered us to be sent back to labor in Birkenau, despite the fact that it was hard for us to move. That meant certain death for Beuna, whose wound was still in a particularly bad state. (…) She died in Birkenau.

Translation from German into Polish by Andrzej Strzelecki.

Source: APMA-B, Statements Collection, vol. 63, pp. 160–162. (Copy of an account provided by Yad Vashem in Jerusalem).

Excerpt of an account by former prisoner Alise Barouch, a Greek Jew who was a victim of the sterilization experiments conducted in blocks nos. 10 and 30 at Birkenau (sector BIa).

On April 10, 1943, I was deported from Thessaloniki to Auschwitz, where I arrived on April 17. Immediately after arrival, I was selected for experimental block no. 10. 98 girls from my transport were sent there along with me. When we reached block no. 10, there were already, apart from the women among the personnel, 7 women from Thessaloniki there. Over the following days, more transports from Belgium and Holland arrived at that block. Later, women and girls from Birkenau were transferred to block no. 10 for experimental purposes.

Quarantine in block no. 10 lasted 40 days. During this time, we learned about camp life. One day, Dr. Schumann came to the block. We did not know at the time who he was; only some time later did we learn his name, and that he was conducting some sort of experiments. Schumann chose 12 to 15 girls from among us. I would like to indicate that I was standing behind my older cousin, whose name was Dina, during the selection. Schumann sent her out of the experimental block, and with her all the others who were not chosen for his experiments. Not long afterwards, they were gassed. I learned of this from the women who were transferred to labor in Birkenau after being irradiated, and who then returned to the experimental block afterwards.

The day after Schumann chose us, we were taken to Birkenau and led into a block where we saw Schumann. This block was in the direct vicinity of the camp gate. We were closed in some sort of dark room, and then Dr. Schumann came in, opened the blinds (Venetian blinds), and ordered us to go one by one into the next room. We resisted. When we observed that no screams were coming from that room, we began going in. When my turn came, Schumann placed me in front of some sort of apparatus. He positioned two plates against my body [probably against the lower part–illegible] and then went into a sort of cabin with windows. The plates were mechanically pressed against my body. I felt very anxious and am unable to say how long I had to stand between those plates. Soon, we felt nauseous and vomited. That same day, they sent us back to block no. 10 in Auschwitz. Over the following days, we continued to feel very bad and vomited, and also had diarrhea. Internally, we felt an aversion to food and were unable to eat anything. After about 1 or 2 days, the skin began to wrinkle in the places where the plates had been positioned. Then the skin darkened, and in some cases could be pulled off the body. In the cases of two girls from our group, the irradiated places began suppurating. In one case, the suppurating burns were so extensive that it was later impossible to carry out a follow-up operation. The other girl died. The burns were worse on the front side of the organism. The hair began to fall out of the burned sites.

After about a month had passed, Doctor Schumann came to the experimental block and asked if we had menstruated. On that occasion, he selected four girls. I was one of them. We were designated for repeat exposure to x-rays. We were taken to Birkenau that same day and irradiated. The results of this were even more pronounced than the first time. I vomited all week. Being very young and completely inexperienced at this time, I was afraid that these experiments had made me pregnant. In this state, continually feeling nauseous, I was operated on five days later along with two of my fellow prisoners who had also been exposed to x-rays a second time. The third person menstruated and was therefore not subjected to the operation.

The day before the operation, Dr. Schumann came, in the company of women prisoner-physicians, and ordered them to prepare us (3 people) for the operation. When I heard this, I had a fit of hysteria and fought together with the others against going to the ground floor of block no. 10. Schumann put his hand on the holster of his pistol and suggested that, if I did not go on my own, he would kill me. The hysterical state was evoked in me by the fact that 4 young women who were in our block had been operated on by Schumann, or on his orders, two days previously.

The next day, I was operated on by Schumann (as the last of our trio). I was anesthetized while I was still in bed. After the operation, Dr. Samuel told me that he had been assigned by Schumann to operate on me, and that he wanted me to live and to remember him. He said that, if I lived, I would be able to have children. From what he said, it emerged that Schumann himself had begun the operation, but had been interrupted by a telephone call. I did not know what had been removed from me during the operation. Today, I know that one ovary and a portion of my uterus were removed. I know that because I had to be operated on in 1962, in December, as a result of the aftereffects of the exposure to x-rays, and this was discovered during that operation.

After carrying out the operations, Dr. Schumann appeared on occasion in our block together with guests, to whom he presented the results of his "work." After we were operated on, there were no more operations in block no. 10. Instead, they were carried out in the adjacent block no. 21. One day, 10 young Greek girls were operated on in that block (21). Among them were two who were operated on a second time; one of them died the day after the operation, and the second one some time later as a result of the operation. These 10 Greek girls were operated on about five months after me.

Translation from German into Polish by Łukasz Martyniak.

Source: APMA-B, Statements Collection, vol. 63, pp. 153–155. Copy of an account provided by the Yad Vashem Institute in Jerusalem.

From a communiqué from the Extraordinary State Commission for determining and investigating the crimes of the fascist German aggressor and accomplices, published in *Krasnaya Zvezda*, 106 (May 8), 1945.

Experimental subject M. Waligóra testified: "Several days after deporting me to Birkenau, probably in the first days of December 1942, all the young men at age 18–20 were subjected to sterilization by exposing the testicles to x-rays. I was one of those sterilized. 11 months after sterilization, that is, November 1, 1943, I was subjected to castration. 200 people were sterilized along with me."

Witness David Sures testified: "I arrived in the Auschwitz camp in a transport from Greece on April 3, 1943. There were more than 2,500 people in the transport, and that number included my 53-year-old mother, my sister with her child, and me. Out of about 2,500 people, some 300 were sent to the camp, and the rest, including my mother and my sister with her five-year-old child, were sent straight from the transport to the crematorium, to be burned. (…)

More or less in July 1943, together with 10 more Greeks, I was sent to Birkenau. They undressed us there and sterilized us with x-rays. After the passage of a month, all of those who had been sterilized were castrated in the central division of the camp. (…)"

A former prisoner in the Chauzer camp (Paris, Cité Milton 9), testified: "In Auschwitz, they placed us in block no. 10, where the hospital was, despite the fact that we were all healthy. They drew a whole hypodermic full of blood from me—for unknown reasons. At the end of August 1943, they took me to the operating room and, under anesthetic, performed some kind of operation on my reproductive organs. A prisoner physician Samuel did the operation under the supervision of Dr. Wirts [Wirths – I.S.], a German. After this operation, I lay in bed as a patient in block no. 10 for 11 months. A Jew from Greece, Beta, was also sterilized. After taking x-rays, they opened her belly lengthwise. When the wound healed, Dr. Szuman [Schumann – I.S.], a German, came to check on block no. 10. He took Beta to block no. 28 and there they again cut her abdomen open—crosswise, which I saw personally. Several days after the second operation, Beta died."

Source: APMA-B, Höss Trial Collection, vol. 8, pp. 11, 12, 14.

Excerpt from testimony by Stefan Markowski, former prisoner number 64914, employed in the morgue in the cellar of block no. 28 in the main camp.

I saw sick Jews who were sterilized by a German doctor from outside the camp. They were all young men aged 16 to 25. There were 20 to 30 of them there at a time. They were operated on under anesthesia as an experiment. After a certain time that ward was liquidated and the sick Jews taken away, but I do not know where. Block no. 10, next door to 11, was entirely filled with women of various ages upon whom German doctors with the help of Jewish doctors–I do not know the names–were carrying out all kinds of experimental procedures, such as x-rays and others. They were trying to prevent the women from conceiving during possible later sexual relations. They also carried out a range of operations. There were cases of death, sometimes after a few weeks. These women were taken to the cellar of block no. 28, and later the corpses were collected along with the corpses from block no. 11.

Source: APMA-B, Höss Trial Collection, vol. 17, p. 80.

Josef Mengele

Born in Günzburg on March 16, 1911, a doctor of philosophy and medicine. Member of the NSDAP. Served in the Wehrmacht 1938–1940, and later inducted into the Waffen-SS. Served on the front from February–May 1943, wounded in combat. Transferred to Auschwitz at his own request to carry out medical and anthropological research. Appointed physician in the Gypsy camp in Birkenau (sector BIIe). From August to December 1944, also held the post of First Physician of Auschwitz II-Birkenau Concentration Camp, with authority over all the sectors inhabited by prisoners there. In November 1944, named SS physician in the Birkenau hospital for SS men.

Experimented in Auschwitz on multiple pregnancy and the conditions in which it arises, inherited traits in twins and dwarfs, and noma (*cancrum oris*, gangrenous stomatitis). Mengele left the camp on January 18, 1945, taking with him records of his research results, and made his way to Gross-Rosen. Realizing when the war ended that falling into the hands of the Allies would be equal to a death sentence for him, he decided to go into hiding. He managed to avoid arrest for a time; when he was finally confined to an American POW camp, no one recognized him and he was released after several months. Soon, in connection with the trials of Nazi malefactors, including the "perpetrators in white smocks," Mengele became the most wanted war criminal. Under the name Helmut Gregor, he arrived in the spring of 1949 in Argentina where, some time later, he became the co-owner of a pharmaceutical firm under his own name. In 1959, the Land Court in Freiburg issued an arrest warrant for Mengele and applied to Argentina for his extradition. In January 1964, the administrative court of Hesse, sitting in Kassel, stripped him of his MD degree in absentia. In the spring of 1960, Mengele moved to Paraguay, and subsequently to Brazil where he settled in the suburbs of Sao Paulo under the name Wolfgang Gerhard. A bounty of three million dollars was placed on his head. The prosecutor in Frankfurt am Main and the Mossad both sought him, as did such "Nazi hunters" as the Klarsfelds and Simon Wiesenthal's organization. A Mossad attempt to kidnap Mengele also failed. Mengele died of a stroke while bathing in the sea on February 7, 1979.[16]

---

[16] The character of Mengele, the „Angel of Death," became the subject of numerous books and press articles as well as Hollywood thrillers. For a broader examination of his experiments in the Auschwitz camp, see Helena Kubica, „Dr Mengele i jego zbrodnie w obozie koncentracyjnym Oświęcim-Brzezinka," *Zeszyty Oświęcimskie*, 20 (1993), pp. 325–389.

Dr Josef Mengele in the SS Hauptsturmführer uniform (1943) (APMA-B, neg. no. 21383/12a).

ᛋᛋ-Führungshauptamt   Berlin N 15, den 24.5.1943
   Amtsgruppe D   Knesebeckstraße 43/44
Sanitätswesen der Waffen-ᛋᛋ
Pers. IIa/Az.: 21016/Ba/TU

Betr.: Versetzungen
Bezug: Ohne
Anlg.: Keine

An das
ᛋᛋ-Inf.Ers.Btl. "Ost"

W.u.V.-Hauptamt, Amtsgruppe D III
O r a n i e n b u r g

ᛋᛋ-Lazarett (mot) DRK

Nachrichtlich: ᛋᛋ-FHA., Amt V IIa, ᛋᛋ-Personalhauptamt, Reichs-
               arzt-ᛋᛋ u. Polizei, Besoldungsstelle der W.-ᛋᛋ,
               Amt XIII u. IIc i.H.

1) Der ᛋᛋ-Sturmbannführer d.R. Albert S a c k , geb. 15.11.01,
   ᛋᛋ-Lazarett (mot) DRK, wird mit Wirkung vom 23.4.1943 zum
   ᛋᛋ-Inf.Ers.Btl. "Ost" versetzt.
   Inmarschsetzung am 27.5.1943, Meldung beim Kommandeur.

2) Der ᛋᛋ-Hauptsturmführer d.R. Josef M e n g e l e , geb.
   16.3.1911, ᛋᛋ-Inf.Ers.Btl. "Ost", wird mit Wirkung vom
   30.5.1943 zum W.u.V.-Hauptamt, Amtsgruppe D III versetzt.
   Inmarschsetzung nach Übergabe der Dienstgeschäfte an
   ᛋᛋ-Sturmbannführer Sack.
   Inmarschsetzung zum K.L. Auschwitz b. Kattowitz, Meldung
   beim Lagerkommandanten.

                                        I.A.
                                            (Dr. Liebich)
                                            ᛋᛋ-Obersturmbannführer

Letter of May 24, 1943, on Josef Mengele's transfer to Auschwitz.
(APMA-B, micr. no. 1613/98).

Translation:

Berlin, May 24, 1943

Main SS Personnel Office
Departmental Section D
Waffen-SS Medical Matters
Pers. II a / An. s, 21016/Ba/TU

Re: Transfer
Reference: none
Attachments: none

To
SS-Inf.Krs.Btl. „Ost"

Main Office of Economy and Administration, Departmental Section D III
Oranienburg

SS Field Hospital (mot) DRK

cc: SS-FHA., Departmental Section V II a, Main SS Personnel Office, Head SS Reich and Police Physician, Waffen-SS Payroll Section, Office XIII and II c, et al.

1/ SS-Sturmbannführer Albert S a c k, b. 15.11.1901, SS Field Hospital (mot) DRK, is transferred as of 23.4.1943 to SS-Inf.Krs.Btl „Ost." Departure 27.5.1943, report to the office of the commandant.

2/ SS-Hauptsturmführer Josef M e n g e l e, b. 16.3.1911, SS-Inf.Krs.Btl „Ost", is transferred as of 30.5.1943 to the Main Office of Economy and Administration, Departmental Section D III. Departure after turning over duties to SS-Sturmbannführer Sack.
Departure to Auschwitz Concentration Camp near Katowic. Report to the camp commandant.

Auth.
(Dr. Liebrich)
SS-Obersturmbannführer

* Der SS-Standortarzt   Akt-Nr.   Auschwitz, den 19.8.1944
. A u s c h w i t z .

1036

Beurteilung

des SS-Hauptsturmführers (R) Dr. Josef Mengele,
geb. 16.3.1911   SS-Nr. 317 885

SS-Hauptsturmführer Dr. Josef Mengele versieht seinen Dienst bei der
Dienststelle SS-Standortarzt Auschwitz, seit dem 30.5.1943

Dr. M. hat einen offenen, ehrlichen, festen Charakter. Er ist absolut
zuverlässig, aufrecht und gerade. In seinem Auftreten zeigt er keiner-
lei Charakterschwäche, Neigungen oder Süchte.
Seine geistige und körperliche Veranlagung ist als hervorragend zu
bezeichnen.
Seine Kenntnisse hat er während seiner Tätigkeit im KL. Auschwitz
praktisch und theoretisch als Lagerarzt bei der Bekämpfung schwerer
Seuchen angewandt. Mit Umsicht, Ausdauer und Energie, hat er alle ihm
gestellten Aufgaben oft unter schwierigsten Voraussetzungen zur voll-
sten Zufriedenheit seiner Vorgesetzten erfüllt und sich jeder Lage
gewachsen gezeigt. Darüber hinaus hat er als Anthropologe eifrigst
die kurze ihm verbliebene dienstfreie Zeit dazu benützt, sich selbst
weiterzubilden und hat in seiner Arbeit unter Auswertung des ihm auf
Grund seiner Dienststellung zur Verfügung stehenden wissenschaftlichen
Materials der anthropologischen Wissenschaft einen wertvollen Beitrag
geliefert. Seine Leistungen sind deshalb als hervorragend zu bezeichnen.
Im Verhalten gegenüber seinen Vorgesetzten, zeigt er das einwandfreie
Auftreten eines SS-Führers. Beste soldatische Umgangsformen, Takt und
Zurückhaltung. Sein Wesen macht ihn bei den Kameraden besonders beliebt.
Seinen Untergebenen gegenüber versteht er es, sich bei absoluter Ge-
rechtigkeit und der erforderlichen Strenge durchzusetzen, ist dabei
aber ausserordentlich geachtet und beliebt.
Nach Art seines Auftretens, seinen dienstlichen Leistungen und seiner
Einstellung, zeigt Dr.M. weltanschaulich absolute Festigung und
Reife. Er ist katholisch.
Sein Vortrag ist frei, ungebunden, überzeugend und lebhaft.
Vor dem Feinde hat er sich während des Ostfeldzuges von Juni 1941
bis Juni 1943 glänzend bewährt. Er wurde mit dem EK I, dem EK II
sowie mit der Ostmedaille ausgezeichnet. Ausserdem wurde ihm das
Verwundetenabzeichen schwarz, die Medaille f. dtsch. Volkspflege
verliehen.
In gewissenhaftester ärztlicher Pflichterfüllung hat er sich bei der
Seuchenbekämpfung in Auschwitz eine Fleckfiebererkrankung zugezogen.
Auf Grund seiner besonderen Leistungen, wurde ihm das Kriegsverdienst-
kreuz II.Kl. m/Schw. verliehen.
Besondere Kenntnisse besitzt Dr.M. neben seinem ärztlichen Wissen noch
als Anthropologe. Er erscheint für jede anderweitige Verwendung und
auch für die nächsthöhere Verwendung durchaus geeignet.

Er ist nicht bestraft.
Als SS-Arzt ist er überall beliebt und geachtet.

                                        SS-Hauptsturmführer
                                        u.Standortarzt.

**Letter of reference for Dr. Josef Mengele by Auschwitz SS-Standorta-
rzt Eduard Wirths.** (APMA-B, micr. no. 1613/93).

Translation:

Auschwitz, 19.8.1944

SS-Standortarzt
A U S C H W I T Z.

Assessment of
SS-Hauptsturmführer (R) Dr. Josef Mengele
b. 16.3.1911SS-Nr 317 885

SS-Hauptsturmführer Dr. Josef Menele has served in the office of the SS-Standortarzt Auschwitz from 30.5.1943. Dr M. is an open and honest man, of strong character.

He is absolutely trustworthy, frank, and straightforward.

In his behavior there are no signs of character defects or bad habits.

His spiritual and physical predisposition must be defined as simply exceptional.

He has used his skills to practical and theoretical benefit during his duties as a camp physician at Auschwitz Concentration Camp when fighting dangerous epidemics. He has met all the tasks assigned to him with understanding, persistence, and energy–often in incredibly difficult conditions–to the fullest possible satisfaction of his superiors, showing himself to be a man who can deal with any situation. Furthermore, as an anthropologist, he has exceptionally zealously made use of the small amount of free time available to him after work to further his education and, in his work, he has appreciated the research material available to him in connection with his duties and made a significant contribution to anthropological knowledge. This is another reason to regard his accomplishments as outstanding.

In relation to his superiors, he exhibits the irreproachable behavior of an SS leader, impeccable soldiers' manners, tact, and restraint. His personal style has made him exceptionally popular among his colleagues. In relation to his subordinates, he is capable of putting his views into action while maintaining absolute justice and the required strictness, and still remaining unusually respected and liked.

In his behavior, his accomplishments, and his approach, Dr. Mengele demonstrates absolute reliability and maturity from the ideological point of view. He is a Catholic.

His manner of speaking is free, unforced, convincing, and lively.

On the battlefield, he faced the enemy during combat on the eastern front, from June 1941 to June 1943, with exceptional courage. He was decorated with the Iron Cross First Class, the Iron Cross Second Class, and the eastern front medal.

Aside from that, he was honored with the black insignia for the wounds he suffered and the German social welfare medal.

In the course of admirably fulfilling his medical duties while combating the epidemic in Auschwitz, he contracted typhus.

He was awarded the War Cross of Service Second Class with Swords for his special accomplishments.

Dr. Mengele–aside from his medical knowledge–possesses special skills as an anthropologist.

He is suited for any kind of service, including any kind of higher position.

He has no criminal record.

He is universally liked and respected as an SS doctor.

SS-Hauptsturmführer and SS Head Physician
E. Wirths
(signature illegible)

```
K. L. Auschwitz                        Auschwitz, den 16. April 1943
K. L. Zahnstation.

        Betrifft: Angeordnete Untersuchung der Zwillinge aus dem
                  Z.- Lager Birkenau.
        Bezug   : Ohne
        Anlagen : Keine

        An

        1. Schutzhaftlagerführer
        ℍ - Standortarzt

        A u s c h w i t z

        Am 15.4.1943 wurden wie angeordnet bei nachstehenden Z.-
        Häftlingen Untersuchungen vorgenommen sowie Modelle der
        Zähne genommen :

        1.   Z    4636   Dewus Margot          geb.  25. 2.27
             Z    4637   Dewus Elfriede          "   25. 2.27

        2.   Z    2381   Behrends Frinka          "   19. 4.21
             Z    2383   Behrends Johann          "   19. 4.21

        3.   Z    5645   Ernst Karl               "   12. 3.1o
            113336   Ernst Hermann               "   12. 3.1o

        4.   Z    5618   Adler Konrad             "    8. 1.36 (Röntger
             Z    5619   Adler Andreas            "    8. 1.36 aufnahme

        5.   Z    2632   Kreutz Johanna           "    9.1o.76
             Z    266o   Kreutz Elise             "    9.1o.76

        6.   Z    5751   Pohl Alfred              "    6.11.31
             Z    5752   Pohl Fritz               "    6.11.31

        7.   Z    5278   Halonek Drachomie        "   14. 5.36
             Z    5277   Halonek Anna             "   14. 5.36

        8.   Z    4975   Hanstein Paul            "   27. 6.98
                    (Zwillingsbruder im K.L. Neuengamme)

        9.            Einacker
```

Der leitende Zahnarzt
beim K. L. Auschwitz

ℍ- Hauptsturmführer.

List of Roma twins; casts were taken of their teeth. (APMA-B, D-AuI -5/4, p. 52).

Hyg.-bakt. Unters.-Stelle
der Waffen-SS, Südost

29. JUN. 1944

Auschwitz OS., am 29. Juni 1944.

Anliegend wird übersandt:

(12-jähriges Kind)

Material: Kopf einer Leiche entnommen am

zu untersuchen auf Histologische Schnitte

Name, Vorname: siehe Anlage

Dienstgrad, Einheit:

Klinische Diagnose:

Anschrift der einsendenden Dienststelle: H.-Krankenbau
Zigeunerlager Auschwitz II, B II e

Bemerkungen: Der 1.Lagerarzt
K.L. Auschwitz II

SS-Hauptsturmführer.
(Stempel, Unterschrift)

Order to the SS Hygiene Institute in Rajsko, signed by Dr. Josef Mengele, for the histological-pathological examination of the head of a 12-year-old child. (APMA-B, micr. no. 1143/69).

Hyg.·bakt. Unters.-Stelle
der Waffen-SS, Südost   Auschwitz OS., am .... 1r. August 1943

Anliegend wird übersandt: ......

Material: ...Leiche...   verstorben entnommen am ...12. August 1943

zu untersuchen auf ...Sektion

Name, Vorname: ...Ruzicka Antonie

Dienstgrad, Einheit: ......Nr. Z 4954

Klinische Diagnose: ...noma

Anschrift der einsendenden Dienststelle: H.-Kranke_bau des

Zigeunerlagers Auschwitz-Birkenau, B II e

Bemerkungen: ...... Der Lagerarzt des
Zig.-Lagers Auschwitz

12. AUG 1943

(Stempel, Unterschrift) ...-Obersturmführer.

Order to the Hygiene Institute in Rajsko for an autopsy of a four-year-old girl, Antonia Ruzicka, designated number Z 4954. The child died of noma in the „hospital" of the Roma family camp in Birkenau (sector BIIe). (APMAB, Hyg. Inst. 1536/18b – micro. no. 849/1536)

H.K.B.
B. II. F.

106396

502/55

10. XI. 44.

Zwillinge.

URIN, chemisch und bakteriologisch.

1) ABELES, Peter 96   A 77.
2) LEIPEN, Erwin 7   A 342
3) —"—   Paul 8   A 343
4) FISCHER, Josef 9   A 781
5) —"—   Georg 400   782
6) NOTHMAN, Albert   17 19
7) —"—   Fritz W   17 20
8) OPPENHEIMER, Jaros 3   1766
9) —"—   Sigmund   1767
10) FEINGOLD, Jakob 5   2048
11) KLEINMAN, Josef 6   8458
12) ADLER, Mona 7   7739
13) STOLZ, Zdenek 8   147673
14) SALUS, Georg 9   147689
16) x —"—   Ladislaus 0   147690
16) STEINER, Zelenek 1   147742
17) —"—   Georg 2   147743
18) HELLER, Paul 3   148578
19) —"—   Peter 4   148580
20) SÜSSER, Fritz 5   168786
21) Zutman, Rene 6   169061

22) SEINER, Milan 7   169094
23) KAFKA, Otto 8   170377
24) KESTR, Friedr. 9   170450
25) LEBENHART, Guy 2 0   170574
26) SCHÖN, Richard 1   170799
27) —"—   Robert W   170800
28) SÜSSER, Hans 3   170894

28 Einpola K. P. S.

Order to the SS Hygiene Institute in Rajsko, dated November 10, 1944, for analysis of the urine of 28 twins. (APMA-B, micr. no. 1158/502).

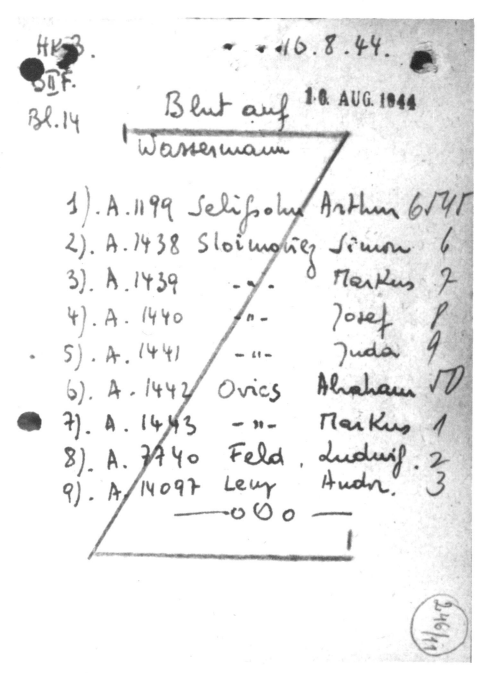

HK.B.
BIIF.
Bl.14

16.8.44.

Blut auf 1.6. AUG. 1944
Wassermann

1). A.1199 Selifsohn Arthur 6/45
2). A.1438 Sloimoviez Simon 6
3). A.1439 - " - Markus 7
4). A.1440 - " - Josef 8
5). A.1441 - " - Juda 9
6). A.1442 Ovics Abraham 10
7). A.1443 - " - Markus 1
8). A.7740 Feld, Ludwig. 2
9). A.14097 Levy Andr. 3
———o o o———
1

Order to the SS Hygiene Institute in Rajsko for analysis of the blood of 9 Jewish prisoners in block no. 14 of the Birkenau men's hospital camp (sector BIIf) dwarves or classified as "dwarves". (APMA-B, Hyg. Inst. 11/1, p. 245, 246 – micr. no. 803/245).

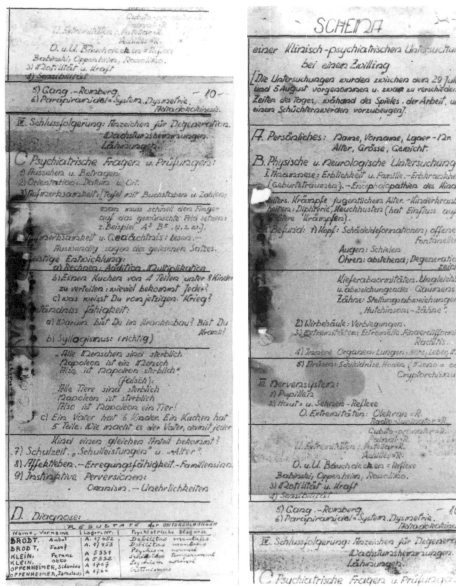

First page of the clinical-psychiatric examination routine used on twins in Dr. Mengele's laboratory. (APMA-B, micro. no. 1525/9).

Second page of the examination routine, with the results of the examinations of three pairs of Jewish twins from Hungary.

Translation:

Routine for the clinical-psychiatric examination of twins

[Examinations were carried out between July 29 and August 5 at various times of day, at play or while working in order to avoid a sense of fear].

A. Personal date: first and last name, camp number, age, height, face.
B. Psychological and neurological examination.
    I. Anamnesia: heredity, congenital, family, and birth conditions (birth trauma), childhood encephalopathy. Childhood tremors, childhood illnesses: diphtheria, whooping cough (has an effect on subsequent tremors),
    II. Findings: 1) skull formation: open fontanel
Eyes: squint
Ears: prominent, signs of degeneration
Jaw formation: unevenness and irregularities of the palate
Teeth: positional anomalies, "Hutchinson's teeth";
      2) Spine: curvature
      3) Extremities: ectromelia, deformation of the fingers, rachitis
      4) Internal organs: lungs, heart, liver, spleen
      5) Glands: thyroid, testicles (mono- or cryptorchismus)
    III. Nervous system:
      1) Eyelids
      2) Dermal and tactile reflexes (Sehnen)
      Upper extremities: Olekran = R. (reflexes)
          Radio-Supinator = R.
          Cubito-pronatex = R.
          Pulmar = R.
      Lower extremities: Patollar = R.
          Achilles = R.
      Upper and lower abdomen = R.
      Babinski, Oppenheim, Roszollino
      3) Mobility and strength
      4) Sensitivity
      5) Walk: Romberg
      6) Parapiramidal = system, dysmetria, adiadokokinesis
    IV. Observations: signs of degeneration
Growth impediment
torpor
C: Psychiatric and control questions:
    1) Appearance and behavior

2) Orientation: date and place
3) Attention: table with letters and numbers; point rapidly to the desired field, i.e.: A^3, B^5, etc.
4) Attention and memory: reading–reading aloud and remembering the sentence read.
5) Spiritual development:
a. Counting: adding and subtracting
b. Divide 4 pieces of cake among 8 children. How much does each get?
c. What do you know about the present war?
6) Comprehension ability:
a. Why are you in the hospital? Are you sick?
b. Syllogism: (correct)
"All men are mortal. Napoleon is a man. Therefore, Napoleon is mortal." (incorrect)
"All animals are mortal. Napoleon is mortal. Therefore, Napoleon is an animal!"
c. A certain father has 6 children. There are 5 pieces of cake. What should the father do so that each of the children gets an equal portion of cake?
7) Schooling: "achievements in school" and "age."
8) Emotional life: capacity for excitation, sense of family.
9) Instinctive perversions: masturbation – dishonesty.
D: Diagnosis:

Examination results:

Name	Camp number	Psychiatric diagnosis
BRODT Antal	A. 17452	Debilitus mentalis
BRODT Josef	A. 17453	Debilitus mentalis
KLEIN Ferenz	A 5331	Psychism normal
KLEIN Otto	A 5332	Schisidus temperament
OPPENHEIMER Sidonius	A 1767	Psychism normal
OPPENHEIMER Jaroslaus	A 1766	Autinismus

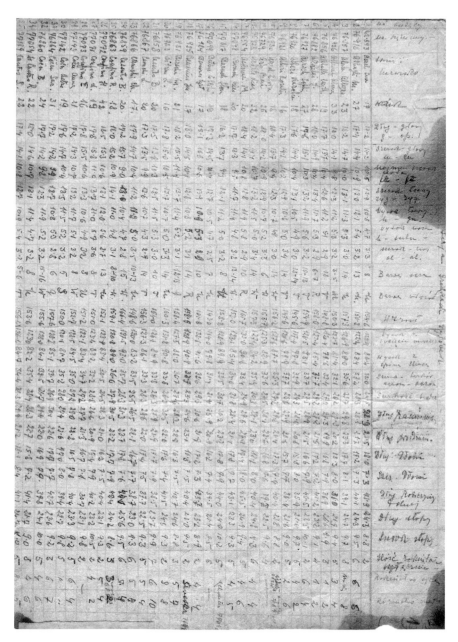

One page from a copy of the results of anthropometric examinations of 295 women prisoners (Jews from Greece, Hungary, the Netherlands, France, and Italy) and 117 twins of either sex (Jews from Hungary) who were subjects of Josef Mengele's experiments. The copy was made illegally by Dr. Martyna Puzyna [Puzynina], camp number 54538, a prisoner with a Ph.D. in anthropology employed as Dr. Mengele's assistant. Along with copies of other documents, it was smuggled to the outside world by women prisoners in the camp resistance movement. (APMA-B, Resistance Movement Material, vol. XXX).

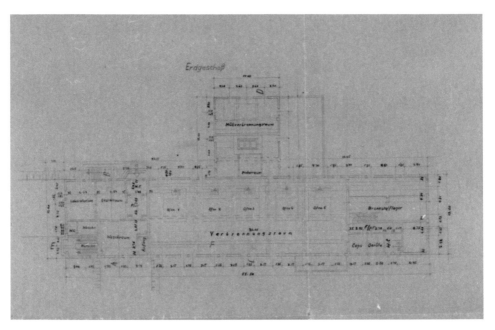

Crematorium II. Layout of the ground floor with the rooms containing the laboratory and dissection, where Dr. Josef Mengele had his laboratory and autopsy room from June 1944, marked at upper left. (APMA-B, neg. no. 17817).

The Birkenau men's camp hospital (sector BIIf), seen from the crematorium II side. In the foreground is the addition to barrack no. 12 that housed Dr. Josef Mengele's autopsy room for a time. (APMA-B, neg. no. 19027/A).

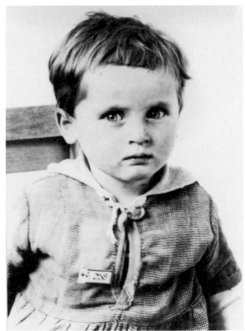

Gypsy brother and sister, Johanna Schmidt 6, and Erdmann Schmidt 7, victim of criminal experiments by Dr. Josef Mengele. (APMA-B, neg. no. 21664/8, 10).

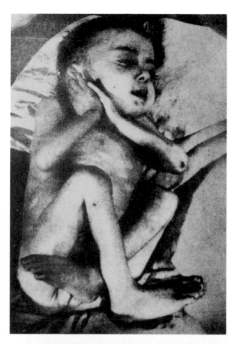

Photograph of two-year-old Lustig Bleier (Brawer), one of two sisters (from a set of triplets) liberated from Auschwitz. (APMA-B, neg. no. 20430).

Photograph of a disabled man, taken by an SS man on the unloading ramp in Birkenau in 1944. (APMA-B, neg. no. 94).

A group of liberated children and women, including Jewish twins and mothers of twins, being cared for by nuns and Polish Red Cross nurses. (APMA-B, neg. no. 604).

Excerpt from an account by Otto Klein, camp number A 5332, imprisoned in Auschwitz, along with his twin brother, at the age of 14 and placed at the disposal of Dr. Mengele.

As for the experiments conducted on us by Dr. Mengele himself, I recall that they took place no more than 2 or 3 times. Prisoner doctors usually carried out the experiments on us, on his orders. They took place irregularly, every few days, on Dr. Mengele's orders. Every few days, we were called in pairs, for instance: "*Zwilinge* Klein should report to this block on this day." We walked to Dr. Mengele's office on the grounds of the Gypsy camp. They called us for various examinations: to take blood samples, to the dentist, to the oculist."

Blood samples were taken often and I am not sure whether something might not have been injected into our organisms at the time. The oculist examinations were especially unpleasant because they put some sort of drops in our eyes and then observed what happened.

Dr. Mengele carried out only the examinations of the clinical type. He ordered us to undress and examined our whole bodies. He never carried out any procedures. (…)

In characterizing Dr. Mengele's attitude towards us, his patients, you could say that, in general, they were "correct." He never beat us, and his name even served, often, as a sort of protection for us. Sometimes, for instance, some capo or SS man would be mistreating us–then we would shout at him to stop or else we would complain to Dr. Mengele, and that did the trick.

Dr. Mengele had a prisoner nurse and an interpreter to assist him when he received us in his office. It was a big office with windows. We always went in two by two. I always went in with my brother. As for twins of different sexes, that is,

Otto Klein (left) with his twin brother. (APMA-B).

a boy and a girl, then as far as I can tell, they only met each other at Dr. Mengele's. (...)

In our group of twins, it never occurred that someone failed to come back from being examined by Dr. Mengele. I affirm that Dr. Mengele never killed until he had finished his planned experiments on living people. He never got around to murdering anyone from our group.

Source: APMA-B, Statements Collection., vol. 125, pp. 124–126.

Excerpt of an account by Lorenc Andreas Menasche, camp number A 12090, imprisoned in Auschwitz at the age of 10 and, along with his sister, placed at the disposal of Dr. Mengele.

They began experimenting on us, but we children did not know the purpose. They took place outside Birkenau. We were taken to Auschwitz, usually in Red Cross vehicles, and we sometimes went on foot. They took us in groups, usually in pairs. The experiments consisted of taking blood samples (dozens of time, in large amounts), and x-raying every part of our bodies from head to foot, examining our eyes and hair, and of course comparing the different parts of the bodies of twins. There was a Jewish woman there, a sketch artist named Dina,[17] who sketched us and parts of our bodies in pairs so they could be compared. They also gave us injections all over our bodies. As a result of these injections, my sister fell ill. Her neck swelled up as a result of a severe infection. They sent her to the hospital and operated on her without anesthetic in primitive conditions. (…)

As I have mentioned, they drove us from Birkenau to Auschwitz. I know that not only twins rode with us. They also took young women for experiments and, as we heard later, for sterilization operations. Mengele was in charge and gave orders, but almost never carried out the examinations personally. (…)

When he was not carrying out medical experiments, Mengele always stood on the ramp at the railroad station with a cane in his hand. Thousands of people arrived by train every day, mostly from Hungary, and he selected them. He was nicknamed "the angel of death from Auschwitz." He always wore a uniform, and looked clean and elegant, and wherever he appeared he was surrounded with an atmosphere of fear and uncertainty, since it was known that he carried out selection and sent people to the gas.

Source: APMA-B, Statements Collection, vol. 125, pp. 146–147.

---

[17] On Dr. Mengele's orders, Dinah Babbitt-Gottliebova, from the sector BIIb camp for Jews from the Theresienstadt ghetto, made comparative sketches of physical features of twins, dwarves, and other experimental subjects.

Excerpt from a deposition on the camp "hospital" in Birkenau (sector BIIf) and experimentation conducted there, submitted during the trial of Rudolf Höss by Dr. Alfred Fiderkiewicz, former prisoner number 138907.

Dr. Mengele (Hauptsturmführer) brought several dozen healthy children, so-called *Zwillings*, to our hospital and began experimenting with the differentiation of blood. What the results of these experiments were, none of the doctors seemed to know. We only know that, every few days, they took 5 to 10 cm. of blood from the children, sent it to the laboratory, and the children fell into anemia as a result of insufficient nutrition and the taking of the blood. Many of these children died. Several of them were liberated.

Source: APMA-B, Höss Trial Collection, vol. 3a, p. 182.

Excerpt from an article by Elżbieta Piekut-Warszawska, former prisoner number 46506, employed at the block set up in Birkenau for the Jewish twins subjected to experiments by Dr. Josef Mengele.

I came to the *zwiling* block [no.1 after the change in numbering; previously block no. 31, sector BIa in Birkenau camp – I.S.] in July 1944. It was a wooden barrack with a brick stove running lengthwise. The interior was furnished with wooden bunks. At this time, the transports of Jews from Theresienstadt were increasing. After selection on the ramp, about 350 pairs of twins aged 1 to 16, of the same or different sexes, were brought to that barracks. Their parents, of course, went to the gas. These were Jewish children from various countries (France, Holland, Belgium, Hungary, and Germany). They were all healthy and good looking, but frightened and weeping (…).

In the middle of August, at high noon, Dr. Mengele appeared in the company of two German NCOs and *lagerälteste* Stenia.[18] After inspecting the block, they ordered that the children, according to a list of their numbers (all the children had tattoos on their arms) should be led in groups, by age, to an outpatient clinic in the men's camp.[19] It turned out that they were supposed to be "examined." Later, it became clear that these were anthropometric, x-ray, and morphological examinations. This was in preparation for later experimental operations, as one of the Polish doctors informed me.

The anthropometric examinations took place in the following manner: the children were stripped naked, and were measured with the aid of precision instruments (protractors, compasses, and calipers) for hours (2 to 5 hours). Pairs of twins were examined to determine if the measurements were identical. Copious notes were taken. For the children, this was a difficult experience. Frightened, tired, hungry, and cold, they got up at six in the morning and walked a kilometer and a half from the barrack to the clinic. Further examinations, namely the x-rays, took place in the same conditions. It was already very cold outside–it was the end of September or the beginning of October–and the examination room was unheated. (…)

The last examinations–morphological–were particularly drastic. Samples of blood were collected first from the fingers and then from the arteries, two or three times from the same victims in some cases. The children screamed and tried to cover themselves up to avoid being touched. The personnel resorted to force. (…) Drops were also put into their eyes. I did not see

---

[18] Stanisława Starostka, deported to Auschwitz on April 27, 1942 from the prison in Tarnów, was *Lagerälteste* (camp senior prisoner) in the women's camp. Rather than using her post to aid her fellow prisoners, she was ruthless and cruel to them.

[19] The men's hospital camp in Birkenau sector BIIf.

the procedure itself, since they took the children into the next room. Some pairs of children received drops in both eyes, and others in only one. I was ordered only to observe the reactions, and not to intervene in any way in case of any changes, redness, or swelling. The results of these practices were painful for the victims. They suffered from severe swelling of the eyelids, a burning sensation, and intense watering of the eyes.

Source: Elżbieta Piekut-Warszawska, *Dzieci w obozie oświęcimskim (wspomnienia pielęgniarki)*, "Przegląd Lekarski", vol. 1 (1967), pp. 204–205.

Excerpt from an account by dentist Maria Hanel-Halska, former prisoner, camp number 38396, hired by Josef Mengele to examine the teeth of twins.

He [Mengele – I.S.] ordered me to go to the chancery (Schreibstube), so that I could be added to the Zahnstation list, and he added that he would bring me books (possessing books was forbidden) about dental anomalies, since he was doing research on twins. He also ordered me to carry out comparative examinations and to aid myself with information from the books I obtained. (…) I began working on the twins immediately. I took casts of them and wrote up a description of every interesting case. (…) I gave my work along with the casts to Dr. Mengele before the liquidation of the camp.

Source: APMA-B, Statements Collection, vol. 91, pp. 25–26

Excerpt from the memoirs of Dr. Miklos Nyiszli, a Hungarian anatomist and pathologist, who was Dr. Mengele's assistant in Auschwitz.

The obercapo of the Sonderkommando comes in. He announces that an SS man is waiting for me at the crematorium gate with a group of prisoners bearing corpses. (…) He hands me a folder with the paperwork on a pair of twins. I call my people to carry the stretcher into the autopsy rooms and place them on the tables. I open the folder and glance over the documents. They consist of scientific notes on both twins, with x-rays, drawings, and the results of medical examinations of an impressive clinical standard. The only thing missing is the autopsy protocol, and that's my job!

These two small twins died simultaneously. (…) Their death makes it possible to carry out autopsies on them, intended to solve the mystery of reproduction.

The "great aim" of this research is to increase the birth rate of the "higher race," which has been summoned to rule. More precisely, to ensure that every German mother gives birth to twins in the future. (…) Dr. Mengele has undertaken the required research. (…)

That same henchman sits before me, among the microscopes, test tubes, and glass retorts for hours–and also stands for hours over the autopsy table, in a blood-spattered smock. (…)

The idea is to propagate the German race, and the final goal is enough Germans to populate the territories defined as the Lebensraum of the Third Reich, from which the Czechs, Hungarians, Poles, Dutch, and other peoples will have been removed.

I complete the autopsy on the twins. I write up the notes and precisely record all my observations in the book. I can see that Mengele is satisfied. (…)

I obtain the corpses of the next twins. They bring in four pairs of twins from the Gypsy camp. These are Gypsy children below the age of ten. (…) In the external side of the muscle of the left ventricle, I notice a pale red spot the size of a pinhead, barely perceptible against the background. I cannot be wrong about this. A needle prick, very delicate. A hypodermic needle, naturally. For what reason did a child receive a cardiac injection? (…) With pincers, I separate the tissue and sniff it. The strong, unmistakable smell of phenol hits me. And so the child obtained an injection of phenol. (…) I have uncovered one of the darkest secrets of the Third Reich. That is: they kill here not only with gas, but also with injections of phenol directly into the heart!

Source: Nyiszli Miklos, *Byłem asystentem doktora Mengele, wspomnienia lekarza z Oświęcimia*, Warsaw 1996, pp. 43–45.

Excerpt from an account by Danuta Szymańska, former prisoner no. 43536, employed as a nurse in the Birkenau [sector BIIe] Gypsy family camp, where she cared for patients with noma.

On orders from Dr. Mengele, barrack no. 22[20] was designated for "scientific experiments" on twins, growth anomalies, and the water cancer [chancre] disease (noma). Dr. Bertold Epstein, a prof. at Prague University and a world-renowned pediatrician, along with his assistant Dr. Rudolf Weiskopf (now Vitek), another prisoner of Czech nationality, wrote the scholarly descriptions for the experimental material supplied by Dr. Mengele. Part of block no. 22 was designated for Gypsies suffering from noma, and there were also patients there suffering from scabies with secondary infections and extreme fatigue. Dr. Josef Mengele visited the Noma ward almost every day. Dr. Mengele was then a man in his thirties, rather tall, with dark hair, a penetrating gaze, and a rather long, expressionless face. An SS officer who always looked elegant. During his visits to block no. 22, Dr. Mengele was interested exclusively in the Gypsies suffering from noma, who had to be brought from their beds–bunks placed along the chimney stove that ran the length of the barrack–for him to examine them.

The pathological process of water cancer involves the loss of the soft tissue of the cheek in such a way that the teeth, gum, and jawbone are exposed. Despite the repellent appearance and the odor given off by the rotting cheeks, Dr. Mengele carefully examined the Gypsies and took pictures of their cheeks with a camera or ordered a prisoner-painter to sketch the faces of the patients. The noma patients received pharmacological treatment and a special, nutritious diet–except that, at Dr. Mengele's orders, their treatment was changed. And so, for example, when the condition of some of the patients improved from the drugs and special diet, he ordered that they be moved to other beds and taken off the nutritious diet. Then the condition of these patients worsened radically and the wounds in their cheeks reopened. Then Dr. Mengele photographed these patients again, took away their charts, and ordered the patients to be taken to his laboratory in the "Sauna" (in sector BIIe). The patients taken to this laboratory never returned to block no. 22, and I never saw them among the Gypsies in the camp barracks. As I recall, there were between ten and twenty such cases. I also recall that Dr. Mengele ordered some young men suffering from Noma to be sent to the hospital in the main camp in Oświęcim. I never saw these people again, either among the patients or in the Gypsy camp.

I remember the following event from the time when I worked in block no. 22. It was the spring of 1944 and Dr. Mengele had stopped in front of the

---

[20]   Barack no. 22 in the Gypsy family camp (Birkenau sector BIIe).

block to confer with Dr. Epstein. A group of Gypsy children from the kindergarten located in two of the blocks were walking along the camp street
two by two. When they saw Dr. Mengele, some of these children ran up to
him calling "*Onkel, Onkel*" [Uncle]. Dr. Mengele talked to them and gave
them candy. I was amazed at this and later asked my friend Dr. Weiskopf
why the children were so friendly with the SS doctor. He told me that they
were twins, and that Dr. Mengele was interested in them for scientific reasons. From that moment, I began paying more attention to those children,
especially because they were well fed, clean, nicely dressed, happy, and
talkative. I would see them out for walks along the "camp street," or in the
kindergarten, where I talked to them. It struck me that sometimes certain
pairs of twins, or children with different colored irises, would be missing.
I thought they might be sick, and with my friend Dr. Witold Kulesza in the
internal medicine ward. But they weren't there, so I asked the prisoner
functionary in the kindergarten, Helena Hannemann, where the twins and
children with different colored irises went. She replied that she did not
know, but that every so often, Dr. Mengele took several pairs of twins with
him in a vehicle and ordered them crossed off the kindergarten roll.

Since I knew that Dr. Epstein, in his room, wrote studies for Dr. Mengele
on the twin research, I asked him what happened to the children that Dr.
Mengele took away from the camp. Dr. Epstein replied that it would be
better for me not to be interested, and to look after my noma patients.

I personally avoided contact as much as possible with Dr. Mengele,
whom I feared since the time when I witnessed the selection of Gypsies.
That was late in the fall of 1943. After evening roll call, the block supervisor
ordered me and several of my friends to go and help the personnel in block
no. 32. Dr. Mengele was there in the hospital office. He ordered us to find
Gypsies with certain numbers among the patients in bed, and take them to
the antechamber of the block. There, an SDG (SS medical service orderly)
checked the numbers and took them to a truck with an SS crew that was
parked in front of the block. I remember how one of the patients, a Polish
gypsy in his teens, begged me to leave him in the block, because he was
afraid of going in that transport. He was so young, and didn't look bad, and
I wanted to save him and concealed him behind a pile of blankets. Unfortunately, it didn't do any good. The missing number had to be found. A total
of more than 60 Gypsies were loaded on the truck, which drove away from
the camp. In the hospital office, they were marked as deceased. (…)

Source: APMA-B, Statements Collection, vol. 87, pp. 97–98.

Excerpt from a deposition submitted during the trial of Rudolf Höss by former prisoner Jan Čespiva, a resident at the gynecology clinic in Prague who was confined in Auschwitz from January to August 1943.

I presented myself as a clinical assistant from Prague, in order to be permitted to treat the Gypsy children. I excised the cancer [chancre] from the children's mouths, and attempted to gain permission to treat them with the x-ray [that was used for sterilization procedures. When I wanted to use that x-ray in the women's ward [block no. 30, sector BIa in Birkenau – I.S.] and appeared there with 12 children, Dr. Schumann, König, and Rhode were present. So that I could not be a witness to the sterilization conducted on women, Rapportführer Plagge called me out and beat me because I had wanted to see into the secrets of sterilization and the sterilization experiments. I never again had access to the x-ray and, for that reason, noma–water cancer–spread in the camp to a high degree.

When chunks of the children's faces and eyes fell away, they looked like lepers. For the institutes in Graz, these children's heads were cut off and sent in special containers with formaldehyde–to be studied. About 10 of these heads were set aside, designated for the museum, and Dr. Rhode took the others especially to Auschwitz. I do not know what happened to those heads.

Source: APMA-B, Höss Trial Collection, vol. 28, pp. 33–34.

Testimony by Mieczysław Kieta, former prisoner number 59590, employed at the SS Hygiene Institute in Rajsko, on jars containing the heads of children who died as a result of experiments.

In the spring of 1944, noma (water cancer) began spreading in the Gypsy camp. In connection with this, the corpses of Jewish people were delivered to the Institute in Rajsko and underwent histopathological examination, with the whole heads of the children preserved in jars as display exhibits.

Source: APMA-B, Höss Trial Collection, vol. 7, p. 14.

Excerpt from an account by Dina Babbitt (at camp Gottliebova), camp number 61016; on Dr. Mengele's orders, she painted portraits of patients in whom Mengele took an interest.

I cannot recall the exact date when SS Dr. Lukas, while he was in our camp [Birkenau, sector BIIb – the family camp for the Jews from the Theresien-stadt ghetto – I.S.], saw the children's barrack with the paintings on the walls and became interested in me as the author of those works. He liked the choice of colors and the careful execution. Some time later, he came to our camp and sought me out. Afterwards, a car took me to the gate of the Gypsy camp, and I was led on foot from there to the barrack where Dr. Mengele worked. I observed the preparations for taking photographs of the Gypsies there. They were brought in 6 to 8 at a time, in small groups. Dr. Mengele was not satisfied with the photographs of the Gypsies. He wanted to obtain the naturally faithful tones of their skin color. He gave me a came-ra, ordered me to look through it, and asked if I could make equally faithful portraits of the Gypsies. I replied that I would try, and from that day on, SS man Plagge–an Unterscharführer as I recall–came for me on a bicycle and escorted me to the Zigeunerlager. I believe that was February 1944.

I worked in a little sauna-room, next to Dr. Mengele's office. I received card, brushes, watercolors, and two chairs. I sat on one, and the other served as an easel. Dr. Mengele brought the "models" in. They were mostly young Gypsy women representing certain regions or countries (…).

On a one occasion, I had to paint the mouth and throat of a sick boy. I remember that Dr. Mengele opened his mouth by force. The boy's throat and palate were completely black. (…) Dr. Mengele was also very inter-ested in those Gypsies who had, for instance, irises of different colors or shades–that is, one eye blue, and the other brown. Everyone said that Dr. Mengele was collecting material in his experiments for a book in which he would supposedly write about the physical similarities and characteristics of Gypsies from different countries. I assumed that he would use my illus-trations for that work.

I know that Dr. Mengele also carried out other experiments. For instance, he applied electroshock of various intensities to a 40-year-old woman from Berlin, an illustrator for fashion magazines and designer, in the women's camp. He was testing how much she could stand. As I recall, she did not survive these experiments.

Source: APMA-B, Statements Collection, vol. 102, pp. 7–78.

Excerpt from a deposition on abortion in the Birkenau sector BIa women's camp "hospital" and the "hospital" for prisoners in sector BIIf, submitted during the trial of Rudolf Höss by former prisoner Eugenia Ajdelman, who was transferred to Auschwitz from Lublin-Majdanek Concentration Camp in August 1944.

Immediately after placing us in block no. 4, they carried out another examination of our state of health. This was a completely superficial examination. (…) That same day, they led us to block no. 22, where we found about 10 more pregnant women. They carried out new examinations in that block, but more thorough. Each pregnant woman was ordered to lie on a gynecological table. Next, a doctor dressed in a white coat and rubber gloves–I do not know her name–examined us internally, in a gynecological way, and collected all the information on our pregnancies. I felt sharp pain during the examination. Drs. Mengele and Schuster[21] were also present during this examination. I was in block no. 22 for more than two weeks. During that time, the gynecological-type examinations were repeated several times. At the same time, the number of women examined rose, since pregnant women no longer feared being gassed, and reported to the hospital. At this time, the number of pregnant women reached 50. We learned at that time from the *Pflegerki* that a decision had been made to carry out procedures on all the pregnant women to remove the fetus. These procedures were to be carried out partly in part in block no. 22, and partly in the outpatient clinic in the men's wards in segment F–in block no. 2, it seems to me. The women in less advanced pregnancy were to remain in block no. 22, and they were to abort their fetuses there with the help of "scraping" (dilation and curettage). Those women who had not exceeded 5th months were regarded as less advanced in their pregnancy. I saw with my own eyes, while I was in block no. 22, pregnant women before they were taken in for the operation, and then immediately after the procedure (dilation and curettage). I do not know how the procedure was carried out, since the patients I asked about it said that they were given an injection beforehand that put them to sleep. I know that abortions by dilation and curettage were carried out even after the 5th month of pregnancy. After the procedure, the condition of the patients varied, and they received several weeks of treatment. The patients had to remain in bed during that time, since they were unable to stand in some cases. The woman doctor examined them every day, and nurses changed their bandages. I also know from reports by my fellow prisoners–pregnant women–that doctors performed abortions

---

[21] Heinrich Schuster, German political prisoner number 34689, senior infirmary prisoner (*Revierältester*) in the sector BIa women's camp hospital from March–November 1944.

in more advanced pregnancies with the use of injections. These injections induced miscarriages. I cannot say what sort of injections these were. The patients told me that they received these injections in the buttocks, thighs, and arms. I cannot give the names of these patients. One of my friends was named Regina. I know from what the patients said that some of them were given 5, others 10, and, in one case, even 20 injections. Basically, each of them received one injection per day, although there were times when a patient received two injections on a single day. Each of the patients went to the "delivery room" for the injections. They returned afterwards to the ward, some time after an hour or so, and then, after the labor pains set in, they returned to the delivery room. The women behaved in different ways after the injections. Some were pale and shook all over, while others complained of pain at the site of the injection. Generally, they behaved in different ways, with some of them vomiting, and others complaining of headaches and overall fatigue. Since I was already highly advanced in my pregnancy, past 7 months, I was transferred along with 20 others to the men's camp sector "F," to block no. 2, since they were supposed to perform the abortions there. The procedures were carried out one after another, and during the whole time I was in that block, which lasted around two weeks, 11 of them were carried out. The abortions were either carried out by curettage as in block no. 22, or by the introduction into the vagina of a piece of rubber, the so-called "catheter." I do not know exactly what this consisted of. In any case, we knew that the "catheter" was intended to induce miscarriages, since several such operations had already been performed. After the insertion of the "catheters," the patients walked around the room. One morning, Dr. Mengele came to the block where we were, and called on the doctors working there to finish up the procedures they were performing, because the women had to join a transport after the procedures. More procedures were carried out that day, and other pregnant women were scheduled for operations in the afternoon. That evening, as we learned later from the doctors, an order was received–I do not know from whom–prohibiting any further procedures intended to cause abortions. Together with me, there were still 9 women who had avoided the procedure. All of them were next taken to block no. 28 in the Gypsy camp, where we stayed, not working, for a certain period of time. Here, we learned from the women doctors that we would give birth normally. From block no. 28, they next transferred us to block 7, the children's block, where each of us waited to give birth. I gave birth to a son on January 10, 1945. The child was born alive, but was small and weak, and died on January 27.

Source: APMA-B, Höss Trial Collection, vol. 1a, pp. 145–151.

Excerpt from an account by Hana Schick, former prisoner number A-7043, the mother of twins from whom so much blood was drawn that they died.

On May 28, 1944, I was arrested for racist reasons in Szatmar. Aside from me my husband and my three children were arrested–of whom two, a boy and a girl, were twins born on May 15, 1943. They were named Jose and Hedi. Together with my whole family, that is with my husband and three children, I was taken by mass transport to the Birkenau camp. (…) I saw the accused [Josef Mengele] for the first time in Birkenau. I did not previously know him. After some time I learned his name. When I got off the train I had my twins in my arms. My son, then five, stood not far away. The accused immediately noticed me and my twins, and asked me about them. He also noticed my five-year-old son, remarking that he spoke excellent German. He asked me how old he was. When I told him that he was five, he ordered that he should also remain with me. I was also separated from my husband then and I saw him for the last time that day. (…)

Together with the children I found myself in the hospital and to be precise in the block for twins, no. 22. I received prisoner number A-7043. Like me, my children were tattooed with prisoner numbers. Our camp elder, named Orli, came from Berlin and took very good care of us prisoners.[22]

The accused remained in my memory as a state official, very elegant, who made a good impression. He always had a riding crop with him and never went anywhere without it. His eyes had a particular expression, and I think that you could tell from them that he was a sadist. He visited block no. 22, where I was, every day. When he was about to enter the block, there was a commotion and you could hear people say, „Mengele's coming!" The prisoner doctor responsible for our block was Ena Weiss[23] from Slovakia, who accompanied Mengele on his visits to block no. 22. In block no. 22, as I have mentioned, there were sick women. I saw how Mengele carried out selection in that block. The above-mentioned Ena Weiss warned me three times that I was in danger of being selected by Mengele, despite the fact that I felt well physically, but I had become what they called a "muzulman" in the camp. I have great respect for Ena and I am very grateful for all she did for me. (…)

My transfer to a different block was connected to the experiments being conducted. We were weighed and blood was drawn from both me and my

---

[22] Aurelia Reichert held the post of Revierlagerälteste (senior infirmary prisoner) of the camp hospital and cooperated with the prisoner resistance movement.

[23] The Slovakian Jew Ena Weiss, a medical student, was senior physician at the camp hospital. She enjoyed the trust of the camp authorities, and former prisoners have made extremely divergent statements about her.

children, and although he did not do this himself, he was present the whole time, limiting himself to issuing the necessary orders. O)n June 4, 1944, on orders from the accused and in his presence, blood from my son Jose was drawn in an amount that I can define as „2 dcl." That same day or the next, Jose died as a result. My daughter died 11 days later for the same reason. Jose died in my arms and my daughter in a completely different block. I have absolutely no doubt that the accused, as an SS doctor, is guilty of the death of both my children. It was known in the camp that Mengele was experimenting on twins. It was also said that Mengele supposedly performed transfusions of the blood of a child who was a twin to the body of a woman who later gave birth to twins. I do not know if this is true.

Aside from research of this kind, Mengele personally conducted selection in block no. 22. As I have already mentioned, Ena managed to protect me, or more precisely she convinced Mengele that I was "a good mother of twins." I remember a third selection when my children were no longer alive. These selections were such a ghastly nightmare that even today, twenty-eight years later, I am incapable of describing them to the court. A rigorous *blocksperre* was enforced, and only Mengele, no other SS man, was present. To this day I can hear the desperate screams of the sick women. Those miseries and laments fill my memory. You must be aware that among them were beautiful girls who had to go through selection and who called out in their despair that they wanted to live. This unheard of and unimaginable situation was made worse by the fact that the camp orchestra played outside the barracks during the selection. I cannot say how many selections Mengele held. He did it at least once a week, if not twice. Until January 1945 I remained in block no. 22 and I was liberated on January 27 by soldiers of the Red Army. My son Otto also lived to see that day; he was suffering then from a liver inflammation and died on February 9, 1945. He never became the subject of experimentation. I managed to hide him among the sick women. The last selection that Mengele held in block no. 22, as far as I recall, was in October 1944. I realized at that time that 262 women and girls, part of them healthy, fell victim. During that selection, as I have already informed you, Ena hid me in a different block. When I returned, the block was empty. At that time, and thus in October 1944, if my memory serves me, I saw the accused for the final time. (…)

I further remember that Mengele experimented on dwarfs. These people came from Hungary, or more precisely from Hungary and as far as I recall, they came from the vicinity of Maramaros.

Translation from German into Polish by Łukasz Martyniak.

Source: APMA-B, Statements Collection, vol. 95, pp. 50–51.

Excerpt from testimony by Dr. Maria Stoppelman, former prisoner number 82325, employed from July 1944 in the analytical laboratory of the hospital at the women's camp in Birkenau.

My experience in Auschwitz concentration camp began on June 30, 1944, and lasted until January 25, the moment when the Germans left. On June 30, 1944, I was transferred together with my brother from Scheveningen prison in Holland to the Birkenau camp. I was sent to quarantine in the women's camp (FKL) from where, after 10 days, I was assigned to the hospital as a laboratory technician. During my time as a technician there, I witnessed the following incidents:

Several hundred women were picked out of the family camp where the people from the Theresienstadt transports were placed and sent to work on July 1, 1944. The remainder, about 7 to 8 thousand women together with their children were taken to the gas chamber.[24] In that family camp, before the selection, was a certain friend of mine, Dr. Gertrud Mosberg from Amsterdam, who had camp number A-4046 and was transported to the camp together with her father. They were both orthopedists. Dr. Mosberg was employed by Dr. Mengele in the experiments on twins. She knew what that meant and urged Mengele not to send her father to die. Mengele, who had moved Dr. Mosberg to the prisoner hospital in the women's sector (BIa) before the gassing operation, told her, "Your father is seventy, that's a ripe old age and he has to die at some point." Her father was gassed together with the others. (…)

In November 1944, Mengele asked to see the fever chart of a certain patient in the infectious diseases block no. 8a, in the women's camp. In view of the fact that the chart showed a high fever, Mengele asked her, „So, you've already been to the other side. What's it like there?" The girl trembled at the sight of him, and he said, „You'll find out soon enough." All the sadism of that perpetrator can be seen in a few examples. As is known, that doctor experimented on twins, which was his favorite pastime. As absurd as it might seem, he performed various kinds of transfusions on twins with matching blood groups. He did not perform cross-transfusions. In most

---

[24] The family camp for Jews from the Theresienstadt ghetto/camp was founded in September 1943 in sector BIIb in Birkenau. Over a period of 10 months it held about 18,000 men, women, and children. It was liquidated in two stages in March and July 1944. On the night of March 8/9, about 3,800 people were killed in the gas chamber. On orders from Dr. Mengele, 70 twins needed for his experiments were left alive. At the beginning of July, 2,000 women and 1,000 men were transferred to other camps following selection. About 7,000 people were killed in the gas chambers on the night of July 10/11 and 11/12, 1944.

cases those transfusions led to severe complications and caused terrible suffering to the victims. (...) Human life had no value for him, it was worth the same as any other experimental animal.

Translation from German into Polish by Łukasz Martyniak.

Source: APMA-B, Höss Trial Collection, vol. 2, pp. 7–15.

Emil Kaschub

Born April 3, 1919 in Menguth. Late in the summer of 1944, Wehrmacht headquarters sent him to Auschwitz in order to expose the various methods of malingering that were becoming more common among German troops, especially on the eastern front. These included simulating illness by deliberately inducing sores, abscesses, fever, and contagious hepatitis.

Kaschub tested various kinds of poisonous substances on Jewish prisoners by rubbing them into the skin, injecting them into the extremities, and administering them orally. He succeeded in provoking the same symptoms as those reported by German soldiers. Kaschub performed his experiments in a tightly guarded, off-limits room upstairs in block no. 28 in the main camp.

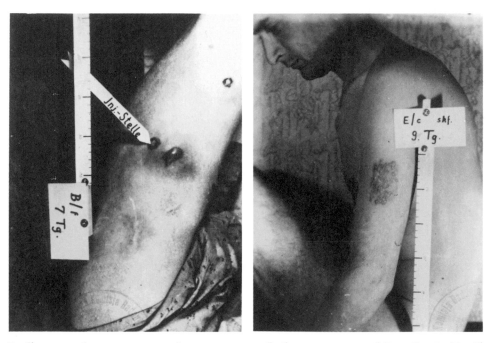

Inflammation, suppurating sores, and abscesses resulting from Emil Kaschub's experiments (photograph preserved by prisoners assigned to the Gestapo camp photo studio, the *Erkennungsdienst*). (APMA-B, neg. no. 448, 466).

Excerpt of an account by Alfred Woycicki, former prisoner number 39247, employed in the Political Department photography studio, on the experiments carried out by Wehrmacht corporal Emil Kaschub.

Aside from photographs of every prisoner, our laboratory also frequently produced pictures of other subjects, including the experiments on human subjects by SS medics and doctors. For example, a certain "doctor" Kaschub, a Wehrmacht *feldwebel* [a senior NCO rank in the German army], experimented on the second floor of block no. 28 in the spring of 1944 on irritations caused by the action of some sort of chemical substance on the skin, mostly on the legs. His "guinea pigs" were cut off from any contact with the rest of the camp and block. Later, Kaschub photographed these infected extremities every few days, in every stage of the course of the illness. Small tablets placed next to the wound indicated the number of days, the chemical substance used (for instance, "Gasoline"), and the dimensions of the wound or infection. Kaschub brought these pictures to the Erkennungsdienst to be developed and have copies made. Hofmann[25] informed us in no uncertain terms that these pictures were top secret and immeasurably important, that he would control every print, and that even the ones that did not come out should be given to him. He personally supervised this work in the laboratory, as well. Kaschub himself never loaded the film into his camera, but entrusted this to Hoffman or our capo. One morning, when he did not want to wait, he ordered that the camera, loaded with new film, be brought to him in the isolation room in block no. 28. When I delivered the camera, Kaschub wasn't there, while the room, exceptionally, was open, since it was being cleaned. There were 20 well built young prisoners there. Waiting for Kaschub's return, I began talking to them. According to what they said, they were all strong and completely healthy before being brought there. None of them had ever had any skin diseases. Kaschub began making scratches on their skin, placed compresses soaked in or smeared with some sort of chemicals there, and bandaged them up. They soon began having painful symptoms, followed by pus and rotting flesh. This was a sort of artificial phlegmon. The sores were bandaged when I was in Kaschub's isolation room, but their descriptions agreed with what I had seen in the pictures. These experiments were supposedly undertaken in order to discover the means used by Germans shirking military service.

Source: APMA-B, Statements Collection, vol. 9, pp. 1319–1320.

---

[25] Ernst Hofmann, vice director of the identification service (Erkennungsdienst) in the Political Department (camp gestapo).

Excerpt from a deposition submitted in February 1945 to the Soviet Commission on the grounds of the liberated camp by former prisoner Tomas Bardij, a Hungarian Jew (born in Budapest in 1923). Tomas Bardij was a victim of Wehrmacht doctor Emil Kaschub's experiments.

I was deported to the Auschwitz camp in June 1944. At the beginning of August 1944, my legs swelled from hunger and I was admitted as patient to block no. 19 of the Auschwitz branch [in fact, the Auschwitz Main Camp].

Around August 22, 1944, a commission led by the chief camp physician Dr. Klajs [Klein[26]] came into block no. 19, where we were. Along with them was SS senior sergeant Emil Kaszur [Kaschub–henceforth in the proper spelling].

During the review of the patients, they chose 20 men, all my age, and sent us to block no. 28, where they placed us in isolation room no. 13. Emil Kaschub forbade the SS men to let us out, and did not permit us to have any contact with other people. We were only taken out of the room once a day, for our needs. The rest of the time, a "chamber pot" was placed in the room. (…)

Emil Kaschub personally took each of us and used a special scraper to remove the outer layer of skin from our calves, and then smeared some of us with an ointment and others with a liquid. He did that with all twenty of us, and then observed us, that is, the process of the inflammation of the skin or the healing of the wound. He took pictures of our wounds every day. As soon as the wounds that he needed became totally rotten, he cut out the infected cells, along with muscle, from each of us, and took them away. Not only I, but also my friends from the camp were subjected to such experiments. (…)

When photographing the infected parts of our bodies, Emil Kaschub placed each of us on a table. He drew the curtains and used lamps when taking the pictures. Then he asked: "Well, does it hurt?" When we answered "yes," he said, "like all the terrible things a German soldier has to suffer because of you filthy Jews."

Emil Kaschub later left for Brussels. During his absence, Dr. Schwarz helped save many of us by giving us intensive treatment and sending those who had recovered to other blocks. But, in line with the regulations of the camp administration, those whom Schwarz was not able to cure were sent to the crematoria and burned.

Translation from Russian into Polish by Irena Szymańska.

Source: APMA-B, Other Collections, 1/1, vol. 2, pp. 75–79.

---

[26] Fritz Klein, MD Member of the Auschwitz garrison from December 1943–January 1945. SS camp physician in the main camp and Birkenau. Carried out trials of drugs for typhoid fever and of ways to prevent malingering in the army. Transferred to Bergen-Belsen after the evacuation of Auschwitz, sentenced to death in the trial of the Bergen-Belsen garrison, executed on December 13, 1945.

Excerpts from the testimony of the French Jew Jacques Freydin, former prisoner number B 3759, deported to Auschwitz in August 1944 and experimented on by Wehrmacht doctor Kaschub.

I was taken to block no. 28, where there was an experimental ward, on August 22, 1944. They took about 30 men for that purpose at the time. They performed the following experiment on me: they used a tiny file to scratch the skin of the calves of both my legs, and both arms. They sprinkled some sort of black powder on the scratched places on my legs, and bandaged them. They sprinkled a different powder on my right arm–the doctor said it was salt–and some sort of white powder on my left arm, and bandaged them. I was in block no. 28 for 10 days. They changed the bandages five times in the course of those 10 days, and sprinkled on some kind of powder each time. They took samples of the liquid that leaked from the wounds as they formed, for analysis. After 10 days had passed, I was transferred to block no. 19, where I was treated until October 22, 1944. When the wounds healed, they transferred me to Birkenau, to labor. Among the prisoners subjected to the experiments, 5 of them were sent from block no. 19 to the crematorium to be burned. (…) The experiments were conducted by German sergeant (*Feldwebel*) Kaschub (…). A German officer with the rank of captain came twice from Wrocław to observe the progress of the experiments. I do not know his name.

Translation from Russian into Polish by Irena Szymańska.

Source: APMA-B, Other Collections, 1/2, vol. 42, p. 84.

Excerpt from testimony by former prisoner [Samuel] Abramowicz Sztern of Romania, employed as a nurse in room 13 in block no. 28 in the main camp, where the Jewish subjects of Wehrmacht doctor Emil Kaschub's experiments were housed.

(From a communiqué of the Extraordinary State Commission for determining and investigating the crimes of the German fascist aggressor and accomplices, published in *Krasnaya Zvezda*, 106 [May 8], 1945.)

Examined as a witness, former prisoner Samuel Sztern Abramowicz, a resident of Bucharest, testified: "I fulfilled the duties of a hospital assistant in the Auschwitz camp. On orders from *ober-feldfebel* Koszub [Kaschub – I.S.], I performed injections and other procedures on the prisoners. I am fully aware that petroleum was injected under the skin on the legs of many prisoners. The second experimental method: chemical irritation of the skin with an 80% solution of acetic aluminum acid (alumin. apeticum). Afterwards, an entire lobe of skin was removed and sent for analysis. In subjects where there was a deep inflammation of the skin, it was excised along with muscle. Kaschub also produced simulated hepatitis and malaria."

Source: APMA-B, Höss Trial Collection, vol. 8, p. 11.

Excerpt from testimony by former prisoner Dr. Jakub Wolman, a Polish Jew, deported to Auschwitz from Slovakia in late April 1942 and employed first as a nurse and later as a prisoner doctor in the main camp hospital (block no. 21). After the evacuation of the camp, Dr. Wolman, like many other prisoner doctors, remained behind with the sick prisoners, and cared for them after liberation at the Polish Red Cross hospital at the site of the camp.
He moved to Israel after the war.

This excerpt from his testimony concerns Nazi doctor Emil Kaschub's experiments.

About 30 young, strong prisoners were taken to block no. 28 for the first time in 1944. The windows were darkened and the doors locked. No one was allowed in. There was only one orderly, and the SS doctor performed the procedures. That is, he injected petroleum under the skin of the patients. This, of course, led to tissue necrosis. The tissue was partially excised and sent for microscopic analysis. All were left with wounds, but in many cases there were additionally severe phlegmons, and suppuration of the entire thigh, and these patients were sent back to our block for treatment. To this day we still have one of these patients in our block, and I believe I have showed him. The wound on one of his thighs is healed, but there is a clear, sharply delineated rectangular scar 4 x 8 cm. where the tissue was cut out. On the other thigh is a wound that is still not healed, even though half a year has already passed since the operation.

Source: APMA-B, Höss Trial Collection, vol. 5a, p. 111.

Excerpt from a letter written by Dr. Laszko Schwarz, former prisoner, on the experiments conducted by Emil Kaschub.

The experiments began on September 1, 1944, and lasted until December, not long before the camp was liberated. At that point I was no longer there. (…) The Wehrmacht officer in charge of these experiments (the doctor, or one of the doctors working on that issue) was Dr. Heinz Kaschu (or Kaschub), about 25 years of age. By happenstance I noticed his surname on his cap when I found medicine, the chemical substances used in the experiments, and also his documents in one of the cabinets. I had broken into it in secret in order to try to find out what was really going on here. (…) Several of the men among the victims of these experiments were given tablets (Tripaflavin – Picrinsaeure, etc.) that they had to swallow in the presence of Kaschub. Others were given injections from various bottles. The names of these liquids were visible on the bottles that I have mentioned; they were petroleum, benzene, a soap solution, and so on. Each of the persons given an injection broke out in deep suppurating sores and fell gravely ill. The accused [Kaschub – I. S.] observed the development of the illness the whole time, taking pictures as he did so and drawing sketches. Next, before the deaths of these prisoners, the camp physician Dr. Klein carried out a selection of them and then they were taken away from the room. The less serious cases were experiments on the upper layer of the skin, and in these cases the skin was abraded with the use of sand paper, after which various chemical preparations were applied and it was then bandaged. When the experiments on the skin had already been completed, the victims were given tablets. The majority of them died as a result of toxicosis.

The persons upon whom the experiments were being conducted were not permitted to leave room number 13, no one was allowed to visit them, and they were forbidden to talk to anyone. However, everyone in the camp knew that fatal experiments were being conducted on young people in room number 13 in block no. 28. I have the feeling that the experiments were carried out for the purpose of detecting malingerers in the army who induced similar symptoms in themselves in order to avoid being sent to the front lines. Unfortunately, I cannot recall any names. One of the victims of these experiments carried out in room number 13 was a young Hungarian by the first or last name of Szigeti. The accused conducted these experiments himself. I was summoned by an orderly to assist Dr. Kaschub in bandaging the wounds, tidying up in the surgery, and so on. (…) I am of the opinion that the accused was not a doctor at that time. He did not have to threaten us with the gas chamber, because we all lived in the shadow of the chamber and it seemed to us that w already knew far too much to be able to remain alive.

Source: APMA-B, Soviet Commission Records IZ-13, vol. 3, p. 362.

Eduard Wirths

MD, SS-Sturmbannführer. Born in Würzburg, September 4, 1909. Served from February 1941 as a physician in the SS K regiment, which belonged in organizational terms to the Nord 6th SS Mountain Division; with the division in Norway beginning August 14, 1941, and later on the Eastern Front. As a result of wounds received while serving at the front, he was classified as unfit for further service and seconded to the Inspectorate of Concentration Camps, with a posting to Dachau Concentration Camp as SS physician.

Head physician of the Auschwitz garrison from September 1942 to January 1945, after which he held the same function in Mittelbau, Bergen-Belsen, and Neuengamme concentration camps. Awarded the East Medal and the Military Service Cross Second Class with Swords. Experimented in Auschwitz on malignant tumors (cervical cancer) and pharmacological preparations. Committed suicide in September 1945 in the British prison in Podeborn (Germany).

Eduard Wirths. (APMA-B, neg. no. 20575).

Excerpt from a statement to the Supreme National Tribunal in Poland (1947) by former Auschwitz commandant SS-Obersturmbannführer Rudolf Höss on the experiments carried out by SS-Standortarzt Eduard Wirths on a method for the early detection of cervical cancer.

The garrison physician, Dr. Edward Wirths, carried out further experiments on the women prisoners. He carried out these procedures in block no. 10. They were designed to obtain material for the early recognition of cancer, and were carried out by Wirths in cooperation with his brother from the institute for cancer research in Hamburg. The initiative came from that institute. During the procedures, part of the mucous membrane in the women's vaginas was cut out, and the samples were then sent to the institute in Frankfurt in a frozen state. Wirths carried out these procedures only on those women who were suspected of being in the early stages of cancer. I observed these procedures personally. Wirths showed me the small spots that, according to his explanations, were the first sign of cancer. He cut out these spots together with part of the mucous membrane and then sewed up the resulting wound. After the wound healed, Wirths released his patients to the camp, where they labored like other prisoners. Every so often, he examined them. According to his own statement, these procedures had a significant result–that is, they interrupted the growth and spread of the tumor.

Source: APMA-B, Höss Trial Collection, vol. 21, pp. 140–142.

Excerpts of testimony by Felicja Pleszowska, former prisoner number 29875, employed in experimental block no. 10 as a nurse caring for prisoners subjected to experiments on the early detection of cervical cancer by Dr. Eduard Wirths and his brother, a gynecologist from Hamburg.

Dr. Wirths's experimental station went into operation in block no. 10 at the same time as Dr. Clauberg's station. Experiments were done on women at this station in order to explore the problem of the occurrence of cancer in women's reproductive organs. I was assigned to this station from the first day as a so-called "*Operationschwester*," and it was my job to be present in a medical capacity at operations and provide technical assistance to the doctors. Additionally, I was in charge of the instruments and all the surgical equipment in that room. Finally, I wrote up the medical histories of the women subjects and prepared samples to be sent to the experimental station in Germany. In connection with this, I have a precise, detailed knowledge of everything that went on at Dr. Wirths's station. In the first days of its existence, Dr. Wirths's younger brother came. He was employed as a gynecologist in Hamburg and worked there and did scientific and experimental work in his specialty. He was in fact the one who decided on the direction of the work done by Dr. Wirths in Auschwitz, and he even performed the first few procedures on the women personally. Once the station was up and running, he left for Hamburg, saying that he would return soon. However, he never came back there as long as the station was in operation. The procedures at Wirths's station went as follows: the designated women were first given external and internal gynecological examinations. Next, they were given a so-called colposcopy, which means they were examined with the help of an apparatus referred to as a colposcope, in order to determine if and where there were suspicious-looking places in the women's reproductive organs as possible sites for the growth of cancer. In turn, the results of the colposcopy were written up in detail, and, depending on the diagnosis, the women were separated into two groups. One group, the completely healthy, were not subjected to any further procedures. The women in the other group were operated on under anesthesia, and small samples were taken from places in the cervix (*Muttermund*) previously identified with the colposcope. These samples were then sent to Hamburg for further analysis. Wirths himself told me that his brother did the analysis in Hamburg. At first, Dr. Wirths was very interested in the experimental station. It was equipped with the best medical equipment. Wirths did the operations and wrote them up himself. Very often, he also invited various SS dignitaries from the camp, and especially Höss and Schwarz, to observe the procedures. As opposed to Clauberg, Wirths employed prisoner doctors at his station. In the early days, the Frenchwoman Adelheid Hodwahl [Adelajde Hautval – I.S.][27], a doctor whose specialty was psychiatry rather than gynecology, worked there. After Wirths trained her, she did some of the work for him, performing colposcopies, write-ups, and operations. Not long afterwards, several weeks later, Dr. Max Samuel was brought to Wirths's station. Samuel, a gynecological surgeon, was a prisoner, a Jew by origin, and had German citizenship. I heard that he was famous in his field, and Wirths himself treated him exceptionally well. You could see that Wirths regarded Samuel as a scientific authority. Wirths even took steps towards enabling Samuel to become an Aryan. After arriving, Samuel took the place of Dr. Hodwahl, who then shifted her attention to the internal medicine problems of the "patients" in block no. 10. Dr. Wirths shifted all his work onto Dr. Samuel, and confined himself to supervising Samuel and checking his work. This state of affairs continued until May 1944. During this time, I made friends with Dr. Samuel and we were completely open with each other. On this basis, I can state that Samuel not only showed no particular enthusiasm in running Wirths's station, but in fact attempted to limit himself to the most essential things. I know, for example, that Wirths ordered Samuel to carry out 4 operations per day. However, Samuel never carried out that amount, on the pretext that it was technically impossible, even though he could in fact have carried out that many procedures and even more. In connection with his work at Wirths's experimental station, Samuel even wrote several scientific articles on gynecological subjects. There were cases when Samuel was called at Clauberg's station by Oberscharführer Binning, who was employed there. As a result, Samuel got into an argument with Binning in the presence of Wirths in May 1944, and was shot by the camp authorities as a result.[28] They stopped operating on women at Wirths's station some 2 months before that, and only gave them gynecological and colposcope examinations. By this time, Wirths showed little interest in the station and, as opposed to the preceding years, never mentioned his brother in Hamburg. (…).

At Clauberg's station, procedures were sometimes carried out several times on the same woman. This never happened at Wirths's station. Procedures were carried out on women only once. According to my calculations, at most approximately 250 women were subjected to procedures in this way at Wirths's station. All the procedures connected with the removal of samples from the cervix were performed under anesthesia (Evipan). If

---

[27] Dr. Adelajde Hautval, from France, employed as a prisoner doctor in the camp hospital, refused to collaborate in experiments conducted by Nazi doctors; later transerred from Auschwitz to Ravensbrück.

[28] Killed in the gas chamber according to other prisoners.

a woman could not be put to sleep, she was not operated on. None of the operations ended in death. After the operation, the patient remained in the hospital ward for about 10 days, after which, having recovered, she went to the general residential room upstairs. Shortly afterwards, in turn, she was sent to the women's camp in Birkenau.

Source: APMA-B, Höss Trial Collection, vol. 7, pp. 78–83.

Excerpt from testimony by Alina Białostocka [at camp under the name Brewda], former prisoner number 62761, transferred from Lublin-Majdanek Concentration Camp to Auschwitz and employed at experimental block no. 10 in the main camp, where, as a gynecologist-surgeon, she held for a time the post of chief block doctor with the rights of block supervisor.

The Hauptsturmführer-gynecologist, Dr. Eduard Wirths from the Rhineland, also ran an experimental station in block no. 10 from April 1943. Until September 1943, Wirths's assistant was a prisoner of Jewish nationality and a professor at Breslau [Wrocław] University, Dr. Samuel, who was gassed in January or February 1944. In the early days of the station, Wirths was assisted by a French prisoner, Dr. Adelheid Hodwal [Adelajde Hautval – I.S.], who refused after two weeks to carry out procedures and was sent as a punishment to Birkenau and forbidden to practice medicine for a certain time. Dr. Wirths's experiments consisted of excising (removing) the cervix in order to study the earlier stages of cancer. The smallest lesion in the vaginal part of the uterus served as a reason for carrying out the procedure. After the experimental procedures, the patients were discharged from the experimental block. The excised parts of the cervix were threaded on a string, preserved, and sent to Hamburg for microscopic analysis. At the time when I arrived in Auschwitz (September 22, 1943), the station was no longer operating in the sense of carrying out procedures. (…)

In January of February 1944, Wirths opened a ward in block no. 10 for patients with typhus and scabies. He ordered that 12 women prisoners suffering from typhus be brought there from Birkenau. (…) Wirths personally gave them intravenous injections of a liquid that smelled of bitter almonds, and judging by the smell it was a weak solution of potassium cyanide. One of the patients died from post-typhus complications.

At the same time, women prisoners suffering from scabies were placed in Wirths's ward. (…) Wirths ordered them to be swabbed with a secret liquid that smelled of potassium cyanide. (…)

A Jewish prisoner pharmacist named Strauch carried out a secret analysis that showed that the preparation was a 1:10,000 solution of potassium cyanide. We wiped the patients with water. We reported to Wirths that the preparation was ineffective, and since it was February 1944 and there was uneasiness about the approaching front lines, the experiment was discontinued and we carried on with normal treatment.

Source: APMA-B, Höss Trial Collection, vol. 17, pp. 63–64.

Excerpt from a statement by SS-Untersturmführer Johann Paul Kremer, MD, Ph.D., Auschwitz camp physician, on pharmacological experiments involving prisoners suffering from typhus.

The garrison physician (*Standortarzt*) Eduard Wirths supplied me with a large container with no label, full of a dark brown liquid, and showed me a letter he had obtained from his superiors in Berlin. He ordered me to administer one tablespoon of that liquid three times a day to prisoners with typhus. The letter that Wirths showed me indicated that some druggist had produced this preparation, and its effectiveness in cases of typhus was to be tested. Wirths indicated that, after testing the effectiveness of this preparation, I should present him with my opinion on the matter (*Gutachten*). As far as I recall, I ordered prisoner doctors to administer that preparation to prisoners as Dr. Wirths had recommended–that is, one tablespoon 3 times a day. This test was carried out on 6 typhus cases. These patients were observed precisely, and especially rashes and temperature, but it was not found that the course of the disease was any different from cases in which the preparation was not administered. I reported this result to Wirths. According to my observation, the preparation did not possess any medicinal properties but, on the other hand, it was not poisonous, either. It was tasteless and did not have any particular smell. I did not analyze its ingredients before administering it to sick prisoners, but limited myself to smelling and tasting it, and since it seemed to me on this basis to be a harmless preparation, I had no reservations about giving it to prisoners. This preparation was not tested on SS men.

Source: APMA-B, Trial of the Auschwitz Garrison, vol. 59, pp. 22–23.

Bruno Weber

SS-Hauptsturmführer Bruno Nikolaus Maria Weber, MD Born May 21, 1915 in Trier. Served in the Wehrmacht until 1942, when he was transferred to the Waffen-SS. Named director of the Oświęcim branch of the Waffen-SS and Police Central Hygiene Institute in April 1943, and held this position until the evacuation of the camp. Also served on a temporary basis as camp physician in the men's quarantine camp in Birkenau (sector BIIa). His medical experiments concerned typhus, malaria, the use of narcotics during interrogation, and the agglutination of red blood corpuscles. Died in September 1956 in Homberg on the Saar.

Excerpt from testimony by Dr. Bruno Weber in Minden on October 26, 1946 to representatives of the Polish Mission for the Investigation of War Crimes.

I was sent to Poland in May 1943 as an auxiliary physician with the rank of Waffen-SS second lieutenant and assigned to set up a bacteriological Research Station for Silesia and western Poland. It was located in Rajsko, which lies about 7 kilometers from Oświęcim. In terms of the concentration camp in Oświęcim (Auschwitz), I basically had nothing to do with it. Nor did I come under the authority of its commandant. I did indeed call on him personally, but I did so for the purpose of visiting the places in the camp where my prisoners were housed. Namely, I employed about 80–90 prisoners, who were doctors and laboratory technicians, and there were also several external workers, of whom about half were Poles, mostly of Jewish origins.

In February 1944, I was again transferred to Berlin. However, I traveled to Rajsko from time to time in order to carry out further supervisory work. I was there for the last time in January 1945, for several days, in order to rescue my things, since the front lines were close to Auschwitz. I then had Dr. Hans Münch under my command; he worked independently in my absence. (…)

Furthermore, I know that Professor Clauberg was employed in the Auschwitz camp. He came from Königsberg [now Kaliningrad] and, as far as I know, lived in Königshütte [now Chorzów]. I did not know him personally, but I learned from the prisoners that he carried out sterilization experiments.

Johann Schwarzhuber was the Birkenau camp director, but I never had any dealings with him.

Doctor Eduard Wirths, Hauptsturmführer, held the post of garrison physician. He was responsible for all medical and hygienic matters in the camp. He reported to Dr. Loling in Oranienburg. I had no official connections with Dr. Wirths. When a transfusion was being prepared, or when they were "typing blood groups" in the army, I ordered this to be carried out in my institute.

If garrison physician Wirths desired to have a blood group typed, that could be done in a similar way. In terms of the purpose of these undertakings, I personally did not have to worry about that, since it was a normal medical procedure. Never, in any way, did I personally violate humanitarian considerations.

I never gave any injections or carried out any experiments intended to harm people.

As far as criminal experiments that could be harmful to the human organism, and in particular cause harm or lead to death, and that were connected with the work of my Institute–I never heard of any such thing.

I acknowledge that injections that were harmful or caused death were carried out on the grounds of the concentration camp. Only after capitulation did I learn any details about this from prisoners.

I regard myself as innocent. Indeed, I constantly worked for the sake of the health of the prisoners.

Source: APMA-B, Höss Trial Collection, vol. 16, pp. 101–103.

Excerpt from a deposition submitted during the trial of Rudolf Höss by Mieczysław Kieta, former prisoner number 59590, employed in the SS Hygiene Institute in Rajsko.

I ended up at that Institute by chance. They needed a person who could type. (…) When Weber learned that I was a Pole, he made a face, but accepted me in the end. At first, that Institute was located in block no. 10. (…)

Right after Easter 1943, our laboratory was transferred to Rajsko, 5 km. from the camp. (…)

The main purpose of the institute was experimentation. Weber wanted to come up with a new method for determining blood groups. It was to be much simpler and better than those in use. He was trying to separate the globulins from the blood in order to avoid using serum in liquid form. (…)

A significant amount of blood, not animal but human, was needed to separate the globulins. For this reason, the SS garrison who were part of the institute traveled once or twice a week to block no. 11, where they attended the shootings and placed bottles or jars under the corpses as they cooled, and then sealed those jars in gauze and cotton wool, and delivered them to the laboratory. The blood was next placed in a centrifuge, and that serum was turned into globulin.

Aside from this, the largest department, the mainstay of the institute, was the bacteriology laboratory. It had a whole range of bacteria cultures, from scarlet fever through all varieties of typhus. In order to create the appropriate conditions for the growth of these bacteria. (…) A medium was needed. For this purpose, Weber traveled once or twice a week with Unterscharführer Fugger[29] and Fabel,[30] with buckets covered with gauze, to crematorium I and later to block no. 11, and they returned with those buckets full of meat. At first, we did not realize what kind of meat this was. It was regular cuts of meat. Cut up in pieces, that meat later went to the autoclave and was cooked there. The pure, clear broth from this meat was poured into large, 10- to 15-liter glass retorts. The SS men ordered us to throw the meat away, or said nothing about that meat. For a long time, for 4 weeks or even for 2 months, all the prisoners–we had very poor conditions–ate that meat. A transport of that meat arrived one day and I noticed a scrap of skin on a piece of meat in one of the buckets. Since it looked

---

[29] Fugger Franz, baker and butcher, member of the Auschwitz SS garrison from the summer of 1942; held an administrative post in the laboratory at the Hygiene Institute.

[30] Fabel Johann, from the camp motor pool, assigned to work as the regular driver for the Hygiene Institute.

like pigskin, I spread the word around the laboratory, and everyone was happy to have been eating pork. On closer inspection, however, it turned out that the skin was too delicate for pigskin. (…) I then went to Dr. Korn from Slovakia, who was our capo, and to the histologist, Dr. Jan Mąkowski from Poznań University, and they tested it. It turned out that it was the skin of a human woman. After further examining it, we came to the conclusion that Weber, Füger, and Fabel chose the parts of the body where there was the most meat. (…) This was confirmed by the accounts by eyewitnesses who had lived in block no. 10. After this discovery, everyone who had eaten that meat was violently sick.

There was a similar story involving blood. That blood, as I have indicated, was taken from people who were shot, or from patients in the hospital. I know about this matter to the degree that I had to prepare the required set of vessels for this purpose before each of Weber's trips. If he was going to collect blood from patients, I had to sterilize several dozen 700-cu. cm. or 1-liter bottles. These bottles came back full as a rule. Reports by doctors from the blocks where the blood was collected indicate that people passed out on the operating table. The procedure was carried out with the largest-diameter needles.

Source: APMA-B, Höss Trial Collection, vol. 26, pp. 188–193.

**Excerpt from an account by former prisoner Zbigniew Mroczkow-
ski, camp number 16840, employed at the SS Hygiene Institute in
Rajsko, where he constructed various types of apparatus and laboratory equipment for Dr. Weber.**

I made various apparatus and laboratory equipment for Weber in Rajsko.
Weber knew that I was a mechanic, and he made use of my skill. The
things I made for him included a calorimeter, an apparatus for the diagnosis
of the kidneys, a thermostat for microbiological research heated by silicon
oxide, and other laboratory apparatus.

When I worked there, Dr. Weber frequently took blood samples from
me and carried out some kind of research, and my friends in Auschwitz advised me to find a way of getting out of Rajsko, since Weber was taking too
much interest in my person, and it was bound to end badly for me. (…)

And then–it was probably the middle of May 1943–three trucks arrived
and a transport to Buna was organized. My friends advised me to volunteer
for the transport. They loaded us onto the trucks, about 100 prisoners, and
transported us out of the camp, but not to Buna–instead, as it later turned
out, to the camp in Łagisza.[31]

During the time that I worked at the Hygiene Institute in Rajsko, all sorts
of research was carried out there, including some on fresh preparations
supplied from the Auschwitz camp by Dr. Kremer. These were organs–so it
was said–removed from the prisoners – most of theme were killed or shot
in block no. 11.

Source: APMA-B, Statements Collection, vol. 46, pp. 4–42.

---

[31] Lagisza, Auschwitz sub-camp in Łagisza, founded in 1943 in connection with
the construction of the Walter Electric Plant by Energie-Versorgung Oberschle-
sien AG. In the summer of 1944, it held over 700 prisoners, mostly Jews.

Excerpt from testimony by Ilona Vohryskova, former prisoner number 31496, employed as a nurse in Dr. Carl Clauberg's experimental station in block no. 10 of the main camp, on the subject of experiments carried out by Bruno Weber.

Dr. Weber, an SS physician who was in charge of the bacteriological and serological laboratory, drew blood from women for experimental purposes, always taking several samples. (…) Some of the patients were so weakened by the frequent drawing of blood that they fainted. They were then left in bed in order to regain their strength so that they would be capable of the further drawing of blood. (…) These experiments were often observed not only by other doctors from Auschwitz, such as Dr. Rohde for example, but also by the commandant of the camp, dignitaries, and other SS men. There can be no doubt that among the many unfortunate victims who survived that inhuman mistreatment, there is not a single one whose health would not be ruined for his whole life.

Source: APMA-B, Trial of the Auschwitz Garrison, vol. 59, pp. 48–48a.

Helmut Vetter

MD Born in Rastenburg (Thuringia) on June 31, 1910. Member of the Allge-meine-SS and Waffen-SS. In Auschwitz from October 1941 to March 1943. Initially held the post of physician for the SS units and camp SS physician in the main camp, and next of camp SS physician in Auschwitz III-Monowitz Concentration Camp. During his time in Auschwitz, he carried out medical experiments on prisoners using new pharmacological preparations inten-ded to prevent and treat typhoid fever, typhus, tuberculosis, scarlet fever, and diphtheria. After leaving Auschwitz, he was at Mauthausen-Gusen. He was also SS physician in Dachau and Gross-Rosen. Sentenced to death at the trial of the Mauthausen SS garrison; executed in Landsberg in February 1949.

Helmut Vetter. (APMA-B, neg. no. 23765).

Excerpt from an account of pharmacological experiments in Auschwitz by Tadeusz Kopyta, former prisoner number 2151, deported to the camp in the first transport of Polish prisoners from Warsaw on August 15, 1940.

During baths in the camp bathhouse in the fall of 1941, there was a medical examination of all the prisoners in our block. I remember that camp doctor Entress, accompanied by orderlies, scrupulously looked each of us over. As a result of this inspection, he wrote down my number and those of several of my friends. Two days later, my block supervisor, Leo Siwy, led me and the rest of my friends to block no. 20. I was highly surprised to find myself in the camp hospital, since I was completely healthy and had never been ill previously. That same day, I was presented to the German Dr. Vetter, who examined me and took my medical history.

Several days later, I was subjected to various tests: they drew blood from my veins, and took my pulse and blood pressure. An orderly wrote the results of all these examinations on my chart. I had no idea what was the purpose of all this.

An orderly came up to my bed one day and commanded me to sit up and remove my shirt. He had a small suitcase with him, and took from it a small box, which he taped to my right forearm. As it turned out, the little box contained lice infected with typhus. This procedure lasted about half an hour. Some time after the removal of the box, red spots appeared at this place and it itched. This same procedure was repeated on me for several days. Soon after these procedures, I felt very bad and came down with a high fever; I lost consciousness for brief periods, and I do not know what else was done to me.

When I felt better after several days and my temperature fell, I realized what my situation was. I was terrified; I was afraid that I wouldn't be able to stand it and would die. I worked up my courage and asked the orderly why I was being held in the hospital and what would happen to me.

I explained to him that I had always been healthy and had never been sick. He replied that I should be obedient and not resist, because that could turn out bad for me. The German doctors continued to examine me and became highly interested in me.

My temperature continued to be taken daily, blood was frequently drawn for analysis, and my blood pressure was measured. Dr. Vetter took a personal interest in the results of these tests, and looked frequently at my chart.

I felt that I was at the limit of my strength. I was physically and mentally exhausted, and afraid that I couldn't take any more.

However, they would not leave me alone, and gave me an injection in my right ear one day, which was repeated for several days. I came down with a high fever again and felt terrible. I was often nauseous and vomited, and had frequent headaches. After more than ten days, abscesses appeared at various places on my body. Dr. Vetter was very interested in this symptom, and particularly interested in an abscess that formed on my leg. It was large and would not heal. I still carry traces of it today.

Source: APMA-B, Memoirs Collection, vol. 129, pp. 72–74.

From an account by Stanisław Witek, former prisoner number 9355, who was subjected to pharmacological experiments while suffering from typhus.

I came down with typhus in March 1942 and was put to bed in room 3, in block no. 11. At this time, a German SDG orderly came to block no. 11. After inspecting the sick men, he picked 8 of the better-looking prisoners, including me, and sent us to block no. 20. They put us in a special room there. The beds in that room had sheets, and we didn't have to double up. (…) An SS doctor came to the room the next day. (…) He told us that we would be treated with special drugs that would enable us to recover quickly and go back to work, and that anyone who refused to take the drugs would be subject to what they called "*Sonderbehandlung.*" This latter term meant death. This is how I ended up in the room where prisoners were subjected to criminal experiments by way of tests of Bayer company pharmaceutical products that went by the code names Be, Be-111, or Be 1034. (…) They gave me the tablets at intervals three times a day, in increasing quantities. They were given from jars of dark glass with ebonite caps. On each jar was the label of the Bayer company and the designation BBB 111, followed by small print that I could not read. The jars probably contained about 500 pills. These were the size of aspirin, beet-red in color, and they were insipidly bitter and left an aftertaste that lingered for a long time. They dissolved easily and stained the mouth beet red or amaranthine.

When the Polish *pflegers* gave out the drugs, an SS man from the SDG was always present and watched to make sure everyone took their pills. Furthermore, he even ordered us to rinse our mouths and swallow, so that none of the subjects could hide the pills in their mouths. At the same time, an SS doctor made his rounds, and the SS man from the SDG and the Polish doctor gave him detailed reports. I later learned that the SS doctor in charge of the experiments was named Vetter. (…)

The day after I took the pills, I began to feel nausea and dizziness, and I had headaches, stomach aches, and, above all, pain in the vicinity of my heart. At the same time, I vomited and experienced lack of appetite. After several days, my hands trembled, I had diarrhea and began to lose consciousness, and my legs became constantly swollen. During the time that I took the pills, my urine had a bloody color and I could only urinate with great difficulty.

Source: APMA-B, Statements Collection, vol. 50, pp. 141–143.

Excerpt from testimony by former prisoner doctor Władysław Tondos, employed in the hospital in the main camp, on the pharmacological tests of the new Bayer drug Ruthenol on prisoners suffering from typhus and tuberculosis.

Dr. Helmut Vetter appeared in the Auschwitz concentration camp in 1942 as an SS physician. My medical colleagues among the prisoners knew him from before the war, when Vetter supposedly traveled around Poland as a representative of Bayer, advertising the company's new products. After his arrival, previously unknown preparations began to be used, namely Ruthenol and others I do not remember the names of, initially for treating typhus. To test these new preparations, healthy prisoners were infected with the blood of typhus sufferers, injecting them intravenously with 5 cu. cm. of blood. These artificially infected people were next treated with these new preparations. All of these preparations were products of the Bayer company. On the basis of observation, we determined that these preparations were ineffective against typhus and the majority of the patients died. (…)

I was personally a witness to how healthy prisoners were injected with the blood of typhus sufferers on the orders and under the supervision of Dr. Vetter as a means of preparing subjects for his tests of new preparations from the Bayer company. In July 1943, then-SS *Lagerarzt* Entress ordered me to choose 20 prisoners with tuberculosis, place them in a separate room in block no. 20, and treat them with Ruthenol. According to Entress's orders, we first administered this preparation to the patients in powder form. Since this caused nausea and vomiting, we began administering it as granules, giving them 3 teaspoons of Ruthenol daily for 5 days. After 5 days there was a 7-day pause during which the Ruthenol was not administered. Entress ordered that the patients treated with Ruthenol should be given thorough x-ray and laboratory (sputum and urine) tests every few days, and the progress of the sickness carefully recorded. When any of the patients died, Professor Olbrycht, a former prisoner, carried out a careful autopsy on orders from Entress and following his instructions. Both the clinical observations and the autopsies proved that, in cases of tuberculosis, Ruthenol had no therapeutic effect. This was also proved by the results of treatment with Ruthenol, since, by August 1944, only 3 or 4 of those 20 prisoners remained alive. In the spring of 1944, Entress ordered me to write up a thorough report on the treatment of tuberculosis with Ruthenol. He said that the report was for Vetter, who would be coming to Auschwitz for it. Vetter had earlier left the Auschwitz camp and was serving in other camps. In fulfillment of Entress's order, I prepared a very thorough report. In June or July 1944, Vetter came to Auschwitz. In line with the orders I had received, I reported to him with my write-up. After familiarizing himself with its contents, in which I emphasized the negative results of the use of Ruthenol in cases of tuberculosis, Vetter was very displeased and told me that the application of Ruthenol in other camps (he did not say which ones) had given very good results.

Source: APMA-B, Trial of the Auschwitz Garrison, vol. 59, pp. 55–57.

**Excerpt from testimony by former prisoner doctor Stanisław Kło-
dziński, employed first as an orderly and later as a prisoner physician in the hospital in the main camp (block no. 20). An active member of the camp resistance movement under the code name "Stakło,"
he was in close contact with the local resistance outside the camp.
After the war, he published numerous articles on camp themes, including a range of biographies of former prisoner physicians, mostly in *Przegląd Lekarski-Oświęcim*.**

**Excerpts from testimony on pharmacological experiments in the
camp.**

I was in Auschwitz Concentration Camp from August 12, 1941 to January
19, 1945 as Polish political prisoner no. 20019. From 1942, I was employed
first as an orderly and then as a prisoner-physician in block no. 20 of the
Auschwitz main camp (*Stammlager*). That block was part of the prisoner hospital (*Häftlingskrankenbau*) and contained the contagious diseases
ward, and thus above all typhoid fever, typhus, erysipelas, TB, scarlet fever,
etc. The SS physicians had nothing to do with treating prisoners suffering
from typhus, and only took the prophylactic measure of selecting them to
be sent to the gas chambers. A general selection of this kind was carried
out in August 1942 on the orders of SS Doctor Entress, with the consent,
of course, of his superior, *Standortarzt* Wirths, when 940 prisoners[32] with
active typhus, suspected of typhus, or recovering, were selected from block
no. 20 and taken *en masse* to the gas chambers in Birkenau. After the murdering of the patients, a de-lousing action was mounted in the camp. Nevertheless, sporadic cases of typhus appeared throughout 1943 and the first
months of 1944. Patients with typhus continued to be selected and murdered by phenol injection or in the gas chambers. In 1942, SS Doctor Vetter
(I do not know his first name) [Helmut – I.S.] appeared in the Auschwitz
concentration camp. He first held a post in the main camp, and then moved
to the SS infirmary and next to Monowice and Jawiszowice. He came to
me in block no. 20 at the beginning of 1943, along with the senior prisoner (*Lagerältester*) in the camp hospital, Dr. Fejkiel, and gave me various
preparations, including a preparation produced by I.G. Farbenindustrie in
Leverkusen, labeled "Be 1034," and said that these were trial samples, that
they had already been tested in other camps, that they were not harmful,
and should probably yield positive results in the treatment of typhus. He recommended the application of Be 1034 in the following forms and dosages:
in lozenges 0.25 g., 4 times a day, throughout the entire fever period (13

---

[32] In fact, 746 prisoners were selected in the hospital blocks on August 29, 1942,
      and killed in the gas chambers later the same day.

days), then 0.25 g., 6 times per day, up to 12 tablets per day (increased dosage)–intravenously 5 cu. cm., 2 times per day, throughout the entire fever period, increasing the dose to 5 cu. cm. 4 times a day–[and] in intramuscular injections to the same dosages as intravenously. These various types and dosages were adapted individually to different patients. Vetter ordered me to keep very detailed charts on every case, following a specimen chart he provided to me, including the following observations: the condition of the tongue (dryness, coating, etc.); temperature; heart action (blood pressure); rashes; central nervous system; the filter-membrane system (liver, spleen); and results of urine analysis. In cases where the patient died, he ordered an autopsy in order to determine any changes to organs as a result of the application of the Be 1034 preparation. On Vetter's orders, Be 1034 was applied in cases of typhus, typhoid fever, and erysipelas. Only in cases of erysipelas did large doses of this preparation yield positive results, above all by shortening the course of the disease, while in cases of typhus and typhoid fever, it gave no results. Autopsies of patients who died during the use of the preparation did not reveal any harmful side effects of Be 1034. Vetter personally supplied us with the preparation in the original packaging, an example of which I now place before you. (…) I personally obtained this box, which I now place before you, from the hands of Vetter, and I sent it out of the camp through clandestine channels for analysis. After I returned from the camp, the box was given to me. On the outside of the bottom of the box is the serial number 18342. Vetter checked personally on the application of the preparations he supplied, at first once a day and later every 10 days, and he took away the fever charts. He clearly gave me to understand that it was important to him for the results of the application of the preparations he supplied to be positive, and he put the idea of falsifying the observations into our minds. We learned through private channels that I.G. Farbenindustrie paid him a bonus for positive reports on the drugs. It was known in the camp that Vetter was under contract to I.G. Farbenindustrie. Furthermore, Vetter supplied us with the following preparations and ordered us to use them on sick prisoners: Ruthenol (briefly, with negative results), Be 1036, probably an acridine preparation (with negative results), and a vaccine based on the yolks of hens' eggs (with negative results). These were all Bayer products, used for typhus and typhoid fever. The only one of the preparations supplied by Vetter that gave positive results against typhus was Periston, also a Bayer product. Vetter collected the medical records personally. I do not know the names of the professors from I.G. Farbenindustrie, and I do not know if any of them were ever in Auschwitz. I do not know the channels through which the preparations I have listed reached Auschwitz, but, in any case, Vetter gave them to us personally. Vetter personally infected Jews with typhus through intravenous injections of 1–10 cu. cm. of the blood of sick prisoners, and observed the incubation period and the course of the disease. These procedures resulted in death. I know of 2 such cases in my ward in block no. 20. The victims were two Dutch Jews; I do not know their names.

Source: APMA-B, Höss Trial Collection, vol. 59, pp. 64–67.

Excerpt from testimony by Dr. Władysław Fejkiel, former prisoner number 5647, employed in the hospital in the main camp, on pharmacological experiments there.

I was in Auschwitz Concentration Camp from October 8, 1940 until January 18, 1945 as Polish political prisoner no. 5647. After the initial period when I worked in various labor details, I fell ill as a result of total exhaustion. In the summer of 1941, I assumed the position of orderly (*Pfleger*), and in 1942 the post of prisoner doctor in block no. 20. I held this post until 1944, when I became a senior prisoner in the camp hospital (*Lagerältester Häftlingskrankenbau*). In 1942, Dr. Vetter assumed the post of doctor of the Auschwitz camp (*SS-Lagerarzt*). Initially, he worked in the main camp before being transferred to the sub-camps in Monowice and Jawiszowice. At the turn of 1942/1943, Vetter ordered me to treat typhus patients with preparation B-1034 in doses that he specified precisely, in the form of pills, intravenous injections, and intramuscular injections. I used this preparation on Vetter's orders on about 50 typhus patients who were housed in block no. 20. Vetter took an interest in the course and results of the treatment with B-1034, and came there almost daily. After the conclusion of the use of B-1034 on that entire group, I wrote up a report on Vetter's orders, in which I presented the results. In this report, I stated that the preparation does not produce concrete results. After the conclusion of the trial of preparation B-1034 and after submitting the report, Vetter ordered me to use preparation 3582 to treat typhus. This was the so-called Ruthenol granulate. I administered this preparation, precisely following Vetter's indications, to 50 patients. On Vetter's orders, I included my observations and remarks in a written report that I submitted to him. (...)

As I have already indicated, Vetter was very interested in the results, and it was plain that these results meant a great deal to him. He said himself that he was a scientific representative of the I.G. Farbenindustrie company. All of the preparations I have mentioned were products of that company, and we obtained them from the SS pharmacy in original packaging with the labels of the Bayer Leverkusen firm. After Vetter's transfer from Auschwitz to Mauthausen, these preparations continued to be used in Auschwitz on his orders and according to his instructions. Vetter came from Mauthausen to check on the results achieved in Auschwitz. Since we did not report any positive results, Vetter was visibly dissatisfied, and stated that he had achieved very good results against tuberculosis in Mauthausen.

Source: APMA-B, Trial of the Auschwitz Garrison, vol. 59, pp. 59–60.

Preparation Be-1034, produced by Bayer, tested by SS doctors on prisoners suffering from contagious diseases. (APMA-B, neg. no. 6545).

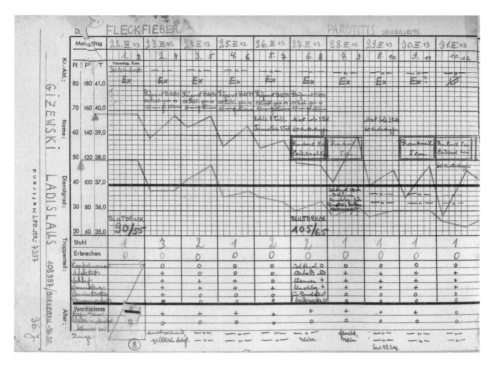

Fever chart of Władysław Giżewski, prisoner number 108997, subjected to pharmacological experimentation while suffering from typhus. (APMA-B, micr. no. 162/8).

Victor Capesius

Born in Reusmark on February 7, 1907. Doctor of pharmacy. Joined the Waffen SS in July 1943. In charge of the pharmacy at Auschwitz Concentration Camp from 1943 until the evacuation in January 1945. Among the stock stored at this pharmacy was the Zyklon B used in the operation for the extermination of Jews at the Auschwitz camp. 4.Like the camp SS doctors he took part in the selection of newly arrived Jewish transports. He carried out pharmacological experiments on prisoners. In 1945, he was at Dachau Concentration Camp. On August 20, 1965, the Land Court in Frankfurt am Main sentenced him to 9 years in prison. He maintained his innocence until the end of his life.[33]

Victor Capesius (photograph taken at the trial). (APMA-B, neg. no. 2800).

---

[33] Dieter Schlesak's book *Capesius der Auschwitzapotheken* was published in 2009.

Excerpt from testimony by Professor Jan Olbrycht, former prisoner number 46688, on the subject of the experiments carried out by Victor Capesius.

In block no. 21, the chief pharmacist of the camp in Oświęcim, Sturmbannführer Dr. Capesius, along with two SS doctors, gave prisoners a liquid with the smell and color of coffee. The prisoners left the German doctor's office in a state of intense manic excitement. The following day, the same thing was repeated. Two of the prisoners died.

Source: APMA-B, Höss Trial Collection, vol. 7, pp.181–182.

Friedrich Entress

Born in Poznań on December 8, 1914. MD, SS member. Held the post of SS camp physician in the main camp and camp physician in the Gypsy camp in Birkenau sector BIIe from December 1942 to October 1943; also camp physician in Auschwitz III-Monowitz Concentration Camp from March 1943 to October 20, 1943. Carried out medical experiments on typhoid fever, surgical experiments, and pharmacological experiments on prisoners while at Auschwitz. Served at Mauthausen and Gross-Rosen concentration camps after leaving Auschwitz.

Sentenced to death at the trial of the Mauthausen SS garrison; sentence carried out on May 28, 1947.

```
HKB Buna                    ✓    20.2.43.    NI-14997
                                                  174

            Überstellungsmeldung nach Auschwitz.

  87529   Friedmann, Motel Jstr.✓      w/ Fleckfieber- Versuchsr.
  93767   Przenowski, Wolf Jsr.✓       w/      "            "
  93841   Kaplan, Judel Jsr.✓          w/      "            "
  93893   Szalachowicz, Morduch Jsr.   w/      "            "
  93895   Szafir, Abraham Jsr.         w/      "            "

  94383   Polkowicz, Meier Jsr.✓       w/      "            "
  94395   Kaplinski, Jsak Jsr.✓        w/      "            "
  94458   Paramolnik, Berko Jsr.✓      w/      "            "
  90114   Salzberg, Henoch Jsr.✓       w/      "            "
  92973   Orlowicz, Jecheskiel Jsr.✓   w/      "            "

  92553   Alexandrowicz, Chaim Jsr.    Durchfall + z.B.
  92782   Rejskind, Aron Jsr             "     + z.B.
  91272   Wienicki, Jakob Jsr.          "      + z.B.
  93562   Lasch, Erwin Jsr.             "      + z.B.
```

Überstellungsliste (transfer reports) from the sub-camp in Monowice (Monowitz) to the Auschwitz I „hospital" for prisoners, listed by name, with the notation Fleckfieber –Versuchsreihe (experimental group–typhus). (APMA-B, D-AuIII-5/1, p. 106).

Excerpt from an account by Stefan Kępa, former prisoner number 799, on the subject of the pharmacological experiments to which he was subjected when he contracted typhus.

In July 1942, together with a group of about 320 prisoners, I was held on the grounds of Buna. At this time, the barracks were already standing there. At the end of July or the beginning of August that year, I came down with typhus. An epidemic of typhus had broken out in the camp at that time, and it also spread to the SS men and their families. Together with other prisoners suffering with typhus, I was a patient in the infirmary on the grounds of Buna. Three times a day, on orders from the SS doctor, Entress or perhaps Vetter, I had to take pills, pellets, which caused us pains, headaches, vomiting, a burning sensation in the chest, and abscesses in the mouth. Whenever we had the chance, we spat out the pellets and pills they gave us.

Source: APMA-B, Statements Collection, vol. 78, p. 7.

Excerpts from the memoirs of Zbigniew Włodarski, former prisoner number 150172, who was subjected to pharmacological experiments.

In late April 1943, I was in the Auschwitz II-Birkenau concentration camp quarantine block no. 2 (sector BIIa), under the block supervisor "Bloody Franek," [Franciszek Karasiewicz – I.S.] when an SDG noncom, Dr. Zenkteler, selected me along with several of my friends for alleged jobs as *Pflegers* (we were all well-built and athletic). Two or three days later, Franek read out our numbers and took us to the *Blockführerstube* [office of the SS duty officer in the block], where an SS man (*Post* [guard]) escorted us on foot to Auschwitz I.

We passed through the gate, where the *Lagerälester Krankenbau* [senior prisoner of the infirmary] was waiting for us, and took us to block no. 28. As soon as we entered the block, they bathed us, cut our hair, and gave us underclothing. The next day, a *Pfleger* took us to the doctor's office (…) where we were admitted one at a time to Dr. Entress's room. He interviewed me and asked about any diseases I had suffered, my parents' health, any sports I played, and so on. When the interviews were finished, they took a couple of us to block no. 21. (…) I was placed with *Pfleger* Pańszczyk in a room on the ground floor.

They drew blood from my artery and finger that same day, and the following day an SS *felczer* [orderly] (whose name I do not remember) gave me a shot in the buttocks. In view of the fact that I was entirely healthy, the interview with the SS doctor and the injection came as shocks. All the more so because they had previously told us that we would be working as *Pflegers*. I had no idea what kind of shot it was or why it had been given to me. When I asked him, the *Pfleger* said that it was an anti-typhus shot, since I would be coming into contact with patients who had typhus.

Two days later, I came down with a high fever, and reddish-dark blue swellings began to develop on my left foot, below my left elbow, and in my left armpit (I have the marks to this day).

Next, I began developing phlegmons accompanied by great pain. Some time later, an SS noncom looked at me and ordered me to be taken to the operating room where, after cleaning the phlegmons and swollen places, they put compresses of some liquid over my nose and mouth and ordered me to count, and I fell asleep a moment later. When I woke up, by foot, arm and armpit were bandaged with paper. The pain was slightly less and my temperature began to fall. Every other day, that same SS noncom collected pus from the lanced phlegmons in a test tube and repeated this several times, and bandaged me immediately afterwards with gauze containing a yellow liquid. Later, a camp *Pfleger* changed my bandages 3 or 4 times.

After about 20 days, I was discharged and taken to the *Blockführerstube* in Auschwitz I. As I was leaving, *Pfleger* Pańszczyk said farewell to me with the words *"halte pysk–rozumiesz"* [Keep your mouth shut–understand?]. An SS man was waiting for me next to the gate, and he took me back to Birkenau sector BIId. (…)

After I arrived in block no. 26, the camp physician in the *Krankenbau* [infirmary], Dr. Wortman [prisoner – I.S.], gave me three days of so-called *Blockschonung* (exemption from labor). This doctor changed my bandages personally and gave me three more days' leave. As I learned, he was a well known surgeon in Białystok. I also learned from him in confidence that so-called experiments on phlegmons had been performed on me in Auschwitz I.

Source: APMA-B, Memoirs Collection, vol. 228, p. 138.

From the memoirs of Dr. Rudolf Diem, former prisoner number 10022, employed in the outpatient clinic in block no. 28 in the main camp.

Entress held the post of SS camp physician longer than anyone. (…) During that time and because of him, patients were given intramuscular and intravenous injections of substances unknown to us prisoner doctors, which Entress brought. These injections led to symptoms of general and local infection, and generalized phlegmons that [Entress] treated himself for a certain time (about 7–10 days) by washing them with some sort of liquid that was also unknown to us, and with compresses and salve, after which he left further treatment in the hands of prisoner doctors. The treatment was prolonged as a result of the lack of the appropriate medicine, and the victims frequently died or, at best, suffered from complications such as paralysis or peripheral peresis. (…)

Doctor Entress applied compresses soaked in a liquid to the skin of the prisoners or smeared on a liquid with a smell that reminded me of the smell of mustard gas. The changes to the skin that occurred in these cases were similar to the changes associated with post-mustard-gas gangrene, which I had seen in my earlier practice. The fact that the SS doctor wiped the skin with petroleum after smearing [it with the unknown liquid] confirms my supposition about the use of mustard gas or one of its compounds, since this is the treatment for mustard-gas burns. The sites where the skin was burned were photographed after the appearance of the symptoms of gangrene. (…) There were also cases in which the gangrene sites were excised. Entress carried out the above procedures either in the small dressing room in block no. 28, or in the surgical ward, block no. 21. (…)

Prisoners with a better appearance and in better physical condition were chosen for these experiments (…). After recovering, the majority were sent to the crematoria. (…)

SS doctor Entress had little professional experience and desired to learn surgery. Since he was not fully prepared and was unable to grasp the conditions of pathological changes in tissue, he brought healthy prisoners from the camp and carried out operations that were unnecessary in the light of medical indications. He performed operations for appendicitis, gall bladder, stomach, hernia, etc. in this way. (…)

I also remember cases of the deliberate breaking of bones in order to master the techniques for setting them with casts or bone screws.

Source: APMA-B, Memoirs Collection, vol. 172, pp. 137–141.

Johann Paul Kremer

MD and Ph.D. Born December 26, 1883. Professor at Münster University. Member of the NSDAP from July 30, 1932, of the Allgemeine SS from 1935, and of the Waffen-SS from 1941. Employed at the SS Main Sanitation Office in Berlin and Waffen-SS front-line unit hospitals in Dachau and Prague. Seconded to Auschwitz on August 30, 1942 as replacement for a camp doctor who was on sick leave; served at Auschwitz until November 18, 1942. Followed his own research interests in experimenting on brown liver atrophy and studying the effects of starvation sickness on the human organism. Kept a journal at Auschwitz in which he recorded each day's important events, including his participation in selection. After leaving Auschwitz, continued to serve as a doctor with Waffen-SS units stationed in Prague. Promoted to Obersturmführer on January 30, 1943.

Extradited to Poland after the war and sentenced to death by the Supreme National Tribunal on December 22, 1947; sentence commuted to life imprisonment. Released in 1958 and re-extradited to West Germany, where he was tried and convicted but credited with time served for his 10 years in Polish prison.

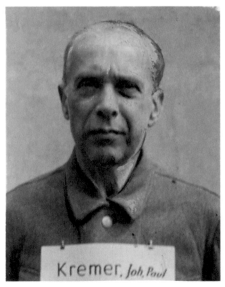

Johann Paul Kremer. (APMA-B, neg. no. 1838).

A page from Kremer's diary with entries from the period when he was Auschwitz camp physician. Some of the entries describe his participation in "special actions" (selection) and experiments that he was interested in. (APMA-B, Dpr ZO/60, vol. 60a, p. 60).

Translation of the text

October 3, 1942   Today I preserved completely fresh material from the human liver, spleen and from the pancreas, as well as lice from patients suffering from typhus in pure alcohol. In Oświęcim whole streets are dropping from typhus. For this reason I gave orders for myself to receive the first injection of serum against enteric fever. *Obersturmführer* Schwarz[34] has come down with typhus!

October 6, 1942   *Obersturmführer* Entress[35] had a motorcycle accident; bandage applied; commandant Höss fell from his horse; *Ostuf.* Wirths has still not returned.

October 7, 1942   Iwas present at my ninth special operation (new arrivals and female muzulmans). Wirth back at his post. Filling in for Entress in the men's camp (admission of patients, etc.).

October 9, 1942   I sent the first package of nine pounds of soap to Münster, declaring a value of 200 RM. Rainy.

October 10, 1942   I collected and preserved material from completely fresh corpses, including the livers, spleens, and pancreases. I ordered prisoners to make a rubber stamp with a facsimile of my signature. My room was heated for the first time. Cases of typhus and enteric fever continue. Camp still under isolation.

---

[34]   Director of the prisoner employment bureau.
[35]   A camp physician.

Excerpt from testimony by SS-Untersturmführer Johann Paul Kremer, MD, Ph.D., Auschwitz camp physician, on his experiments on brown liver atrophy and the effects of starvation sickness on the human organism.

In my memoirs I mention in several places the collection of fresh living human material for research purposes. Things looked like this: I had long been interested in the changes that occur in the human organism as a result of starvation. In Auschwitz, I presented the matter to Dr. Wirths, who told me that I could collect fresh living material (*lebensfrisches Material*) from prisoners who were put to death by phenol injection. In order to choose suitable subjects, I went to the last block on the right-hand side (block no. 28), where sick prisoners from the camp presented themselves and were examined. During these examinations, prisoners with medical functions presented the patients to an SS doctor, explaining the sickness from which a given prisoner was suffering; depending on whether the patient in questioned had prospects for recovery, or could no longer be taken into account as labor force (*Arbeitsunfähig*), the SS doctor decided whether the prisoner in question should be admitted to the hospital, given outpatient treatment, or be liquidated. SS orderlies assembled the prisoners classified by the SS doctor in the latter category and led them away. The prisoners assigned to this group by the SS doctor were above all those diagnosed with "*Allgemeine Körperschwäche*" (general exhaustion). I closely observed the prisoners in this group, and when one of them interested me because of a highly advanced state of starvation, I commanded the orderly to reserve that patient for me, and inform me of when that patient would be killed with the help of an injection. At the time indicated by the SS orderly, the patients I had chosen were led back to that last block and placed in a room there across the corridor from the examining room where they had been selected. There, the patient was placed on an autopsy table while still alive. I went to the table and asked the patient about various details that were important for my research. Thus: his weight before arrest, how much weight he had lost since then, any medicine he had taken, and so on. After the collection of this information, an orderly approached the patient, and killed the patient with an injection in the vicinity of the heart. As far as I know, only phenol injections were used for killing. After such an injection, death occurred immediately. I never administered the fatal injections myself. I stood far away from the autopsy table with jars prepared to collect samples of those organs of the body that were necessary to examine for my work. Immediately after the death of the prisoner who had obtained the injection, prisoner physicians collected samples from the liver and pancreas, which I placed in the ready preservative fluids contained in the jars. I used

Zenker or Carboy fluid for preservation. In some cases, I ordered that photographs be taken of the patients who were to be killed so that samples could be taken from their bodies for me. The camp photography office took these pictures. I took them, just like the collected samples, to my apartment in Münster, but I do not know where they are at present. (…)

In all the cases where I noted in my journal that fresh living human material was collected for me, I was present when the people from whom the samples were collected for me were killed.

Source: APMA-B, Trial of the Auschwitz Garrison, vol. 59, pp. 23–25.

Excerpt from an account by Stanisław Głowa, former prisoner number 20017, who was first a nurse and later scribe in the camp "hospital" in block no. 20 in the main camp.

Kremer was a doctor in Auschwitz more or less in the second half of 1942, and at that time he carried out the selection of prisoners in the infirmary. He conducted the selection in the same ruthless way as the other SS doctors (…) and thus he did not examine the patient at all but only judged them on their appearance. Furthermore, he used noncoms (SS orderlies) at the selections, so that Klehr, Scherpe, and others who had nothing at all to do with medicine carried out selection in his name, since as far as I know Klehr, for example, was a cobbler by occupation. The selection carried out by noncoms consisted of the noncoms choosing prisoners according to their own whims, making the appropriate mark on their medical charts.

I know that Kremer conducted supposedly scientific experiments on patients, causing the death of the prisoner in many cases. For this purpose, Kremer chose sick prisoners from the infirmary who constituted experimental material for him. I do not know exactly what experiments Kremer conducted on the prisoners, but I heard that many patients died as a result of these procedures. (…)

Phenol was also injected into the hearts of patients at the time when Kremer was Lagerarzt in the camp. The injections were mainly performed by SDG Klehr, with prisoners helping him. (…) They held the victim while the shot was given. Aside from Klehr, Pańszczyk gave injections, and on more than one occasion he forced prisoners to help him by beating them.

Source: APMA-B, Trial of the Auschwitz Garrison, vol. 59, pp. 27–28.

Excerpt from testimony before the Commission for the Investigation on German Crimes in Poland in September 1947 by Adam Stapf, former prisoner number 3704.

SS-Obersturmführer Kremer is also known to me personally and by name, and from reports by other prisoners I know that he took part in the gassing and selection of prisoners chosen for the gas. I myself saw one case of a selection conducted by Kremer. I cannot now remember precisely if it was at the end of 1942 or the beginning of 1943, when a larger group of Jewish men were brought from Birkenau to the main camp to work. After turning in their clothing, these Jews waited for the medical commission in the square between blocks nos. 26 and 27. Kremer carried out the examination, and asked them if they could or wanted to work. The Jews did not know what was going on and, fearing hard labor, answered that they were not capable of working. Kremer sent those who replied in this way to the left side, which meant that they were designated for the gas. Without being entered into the card file, that group was sent back to Birkenau. This confirmed to me that they were designated for liquidation.

Source: APMA-B, Trial of the Auschwitz Garrison, vol. 52, p. 57.

Horst Paul Sylwester Fischer

Born in Dresden on December 31, 1912. MD Arrived in the Auschwitz camp on November 1, 1942. Served there at first as SS unit physician, then SS camp physician in the main camp, and from November 1943 to September 1943 held the same post at Auschwitz III-Monowitz Concentration Camp. Subjected prisoners to clinical trials of sulfa drugs and performed experimental surgery. Tested the effects of electroshock therapy on women prisoners brought from the Birkenau women's camp and men from some of the Auschwitz sub-camps who were suffering from various mental disturbances. After the war, Fischer practiced medicine in Berlin. Sentenced to death on March 25, 1966, for his work at Auschwitz and executed.

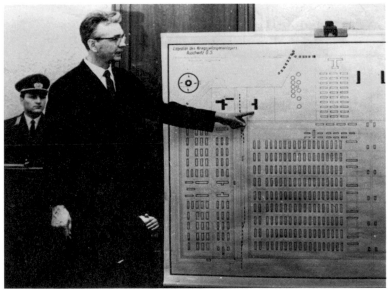

Horst Fischer. Photo taken during the trial. (APMA-B, neg. no. 9624).

Excerpt from an account by Karel Minc, Czech former prisoner number 68582, on electroshock experiments.

The patient (a woman prisoner) was placed on the bed, electrodes in the form of a radio headset attached to her head, and a funnel forced into her mouth. The bed was covered with a piece of oil cloth because the persons subjected to this procedure lost control of their bladders. *Lagerarzt* Dr. Fischer was present in the room. After the procedure, the patient was unconscious (…) and had to be carried to the outpatient clinic. There, after the passage of about half an hour, she recovered consciousness.

Source: APMA-B, Statements Collection, vol. 88a, p. 167.

August Hirt

SS-Hauptsturmführer Prof. Dr. August Hirt, born in Mannheim April 29, 1898. Director of the Institute of Anatomy at the Reich University in Strasbourg. Came up with the idea of assembling a collection of skeletons for the study of racial differences. On his orders, SS-Hauptsturmführer Dr. Bruno Beger selected 115 prisoners in Auschwitz (79 Jewish men, 2 Poles, 4 Asiatics–surely Soviet POWs–and 30 Jewish women); they were transferred to Natzweiler Concentration Camp in August 1943 and murdered in the gas chamber there. The corpses were shipped to the university, where they were prepared and placed in the basement of the Institute of Anatomy.

After the French army took Strasbourg in November 1944, Hirt went into hiding in Tübingen and later in the Black Forest. He committed suicide in Schonebach on June 2, 1945.

August Hirt. (APMA-B, neg. no. 21126/80).

```
ss Ahnenerbe                          Berlin,am 2.11.42    ODPIS    25
r Reichsgeschäftsführer                                •

        An

        SS-Obersturmbannführer Dr. B r a n d t          G e h e i m!
        B e r l i n.

        Lieber Kamerad Brandt!

        Wie Sie wissen, hat der Reichsführer-SS seinerzeit angeordnet, dass
        SS-Hauptsturmführer Prof.Dr. H i r t  für seine Forschungen alles
        bekommen soll, was er braucht. Ur bestimmte anthropologische Unter-
        suchungen - ich berichtete dem Reichsführer-SS auch bereits darüber -
        sind nun 150 Skelette von Häftlingen bezw. Juden notwendig, die vom
        K. Auschwitz zur Verfügung gestellt werden sollen. Es ist dazu nur
        noch erforderlich, dass das Reichssicherheitshauptamt eine offiziell
        Anweisung des Reichsführers-SS erhält, die aber auch Sie im Auftrag
        des Reichsführers-SS erteilen können.

        Mit kameradschaftlichem Gruss

                                              Heil Hitler!

                                              Ihr /-/Sievers

        1 Anlage.
        Entwurf eines Schreibens an das Reichssicherheitshauptamt.
```

Letter from SS-Standartenführer Wolfram Sievers, general secretary of the Ahnenerbe (Ancestral Heritage) society to SS-Obersturmführer Dr. Brandt, concerning 150 skeletons of Jews from the Auschwitz concentration camp. (APMA-B, neg. no. 227/25).

Translation:

Berlin, November 2, 1942

General Secretary
The Ancestral Heritage Society

SS-Obersturmbannführer Dr. Brandt<u>Secret!</u>
<u>BERLIN</u>

Dear Colleague Brandt!

As you are aware, the Reichsführer SS has decreed in his time that SS-Hauptsturmführer Prof. Dr. H i r t should obtain everything that he needs for his research. For concrete anthropological research–as I have already informed the Reichführer SS–there is a need for 150 skeletons of Jews, which should be placed at his disposal from Auschwitz. It is further necessary in this regard that the Main Reich Security Office should fulfill the official order of the Reichsführer SS, which, however, you can also do on the orders of the Reichsführer SS.

With collegial greetings,

Heil Hitler!
Your Sievers

<u>1 attachment:</u>
Proposed draft of a letter from the Main Reich Security Office.

(illegible signature)

Der Reichsführer-SS   Feldkommandostelle, den 6.11.42
Persönlicher Stab
Tgb.Nr. 41/1/43 g   G e h e i m!

1./ An das

    Reichssicherheitshauptamt

    - Amt IV B 4 -

    z.Hd. SS-Obersturmbannführer E i c h m a n n

    Berlin SW 11

    Prinz-Albrecht-Str.8

Betrifft: Aufbau einer Sammlung von Skeletten in der Anatomie Strass
          burg.

    Der Reichsführer-SS hat angeordnet, dass dem Direktor der Anato
mie Strassburg, SS-Hauptsturmführer Prof.Dr. H i r t, der zugleich
Leiter einer Abteilung des Instituts für Wehrwissenschaftliche Zweck-
forschung im Amt Ahnenerbe ist, für seine Forschungen alles Notwendi
ge zur Verfügung gestellt wird. Im Auftrage des Reichsführers-SS bitt
ich deshalb, den Aufbau der geplanten Skelettsammlung zu ermöglichen
gen der Einzelheiten wird sich SS-Obersturmbannführer Sievers mit
ien in Verbindung setzen.

                                        I.A.
                                     gez. Brandt
                                  SS-Obersturmbannführer.

2./ An das "Ahnenerbe"   Berlin, den 27. November 1942.

    Berlin-Dahlem

    Pücklerstrasse 16.

    durchschriftlich mit der Bitte um Kenntnisnahme übersandt. Ich
beziehe mich auf das dortige Schreiben vom 2.11.42.

                                        i.A.
                                     /-/podpis nieczytelny
                                  SS-Obersturmführer.

**Letter (confidential note) of November 6, 1942, from Rudolf Brandt
to RSHA Office B-4 (Jewish deportation) and the Ahnenerbe (Ancestral Heritage) agency on permission for Prof. Hirt to assemble a
collection of skeletons.** (APMA-B, micr. no. 227/26).

Translation:

Field Command, Nov. 6, 1942
Reichsführer SS
Personal Staff

Secret!

1./ To the Reich Main Security Office
Office IV B 4
Personal: for delivery into the hands of SS-Obersturmbannführer
Eichmann
Berlin SW 11
Prinz-Albrecht-Str. 8
In reference: the creation of a collection of skeletons at the Anatomy Institute in Strassburg .

The Reichsführer SS has decreed that everything necessary for the conduct of his research be placed at the disposal of the director of the Anatomy Institute in Strassburg, SS-Hauptsturmführer Prof. Dr. Hirt, who is also director of the Faculty in the Scientific Research Institute of the "Ahnenerbe" (Ancestral Heritage) Agency.

Acting at the behest of the Reichsführer SS, I therefore request that you make the creation of the planned collection of skeletons possible. As to details, SS-Obersturmbannführer Sievers will contact you.

Authorized signature
Brandt
SS-Obersturmbannführer

2./ To the "Ahnenerbe" Agency
Berlin-Dahlem
Pücklerstrasse 16
Copy for your information. I refer to the letter of November 2, 1942.

Authorized signature
Brandt
SS-Obersturmbannführer

ODPIS 27

Amt "Ahnenerbe"   Berlin-Dahlem, 21.Juni 1943
Inst.f.wehrwissenschaftliche Zweck-   Pücklerstr.16
            forschung
        G/H/6   32/He.   Geheime Reichssache!
                                             G.H.Z.I. A.H. Sk.Nr.10
An das   5 Ausfertigung. 2. Ausfertigg.
                                                ohne Anlagen.
Reichssicherheitshauptamt
Amt IV B 4
z.Hdn. SS-Obersturmbannführer E i c h m a n n,

B e r l i n SW 11

Prinz-Albrecht-Str. 8

Betrifft: Aufbau einer Sammlung von Skeletten.

Unter Bezugnahme auf dortiges Schreiben von 25.9.1942 IV B 4 3576/42
1493 und die zwischenzeitlich in obiger Angelegenheit geführten per-
sönlichen Besprechungen wird mitgeteilt, dass der mit der Ausführung
obigen Sonderauftrages beauftragte Mitarbeiter der hiesigen Dienststelle, SS-Hauptsturmführer Dr. Bruno B e g e r, die Arbeiten am
1.6.1943 im KL Auschwitz wegen der bestehenden Seuchengefahr beende-
t. Insgesamt wurden 115 Personen, davon 79 Juden, 2 Polen, 4 Inner-
asiaten und 30 Jüdinnen bearbeitet. Diese Häftlinge sind z.Zt.getrennt
nach Männern und Frauen in je einem Krankenbau des MKL.Auschwitz untergebracht und befinden sich in Quarantäne. Zur weiteren Bearbeitung
der ausgesuchten Personen ist nunmehr eine sofortige Überweisung an
das KL. Natzweiler erforderlich, was mit Rücksicht auf die Seuchengefahr in Auschwitz beschleunigt durchgeführt werden müsste. Ein namen-
tliches Verzeichnis der ausgesuchten Personen ist beigefügt. Es wird
gebeten, die entsprechenden Anweisungen zu erteilen. Da bei der Überweisung der Häftlinge nach Natzweiler die Gefahr der Seucheneinschle-
pung besteht, wird gebeten, umgehend zu veranlassen, dass seuchenfreie
und saubere Häftlingskleidung für 80 Männer und 30 Frauen von Natzweiler nach Auschwitz gesandt wird. Gleichzeitig müsse dafür Sorge getra-
gen werden, für die 30 Frauen kurzfristig im MKL.Natzweiler Unterbri-
gungsmöglichkeit zu schaffen.   /-/Sievers
                                                 SS-Standartenführer.
Durchschriften an:
a./ SS-H'Stuf. Dr. B e g e r
b./ SS-H'Stuf. Prof.Dr. H i r t
c./ SS-Obersturmbannführer Dr. B r a n d t

Letter from SS-Standartenführer Wolfram Sievers addressed personally to SS-Obersturmbannführer Adolfa Eichmanna, informing him about the choosing of 115 Auschwitz prisoners by SS-Hauptsturmführer Dr. Bruno Beger. The prisoners, destined for Hirt's collection of skeletons, were to be transferred to the concentration camp in Natzweiler and, following examination, put to death. (APMA-B, micr. no. 350/13).

Translation:

Ahnenerbe Office   Berlin-Dahlem, July 21, 1943
Military Scientific Research Institute   Pücklerstr. 16
G/H/6 S2/He

Secret State Business!
G.R.Z.I. A.H. Sk. No. 10
5 copies, 2 copies without attachments

To:
Main Reich Security Office
Department IV B 4
For personal delivery to SS-Obersturmbannführer E i c h m a n n

B e r l i n SW11
Prinz-Albrecht-Str. 8

In reference to the letter of 25.9.1942 IV B 4 3576/42/1943 and the personal discussions held on this subject in the meantime, please be informed that Dr. Bruno Beger, an employee of this institute authorized to carry out special tasks, has completed his work in Auschwitz Concentration Camp because of the presence of a danger of epidemic. A total of 115 prisoners were chosen, including 72 Jewish men, 2 Polish men, 4 Asiatic men, and 30 Jewesses. These prisoners were temporarily placed—men and women separately—in the hospital in Auschwitz and are currently subject to quarantine. For the purpose of the further study of the selected prisoners it is necessary for them to be <u>immediately transferred to Natzweiler Concentration Camp</u>, which, in view of the danger of epidemic in Auschwitz Concentration Camp, must be done with all expediency.
    (...)

/-/ Sievers
SS-Standartenführer
(signature)

Personal Staff   Waischenfeld/Orf., 5.9.1944
Reichsführer SS
Office A   State Secret!

23?

Der Reichsführer-ſſ
Persönlicher Stab
Amt „A"

Waischenfeld/Ofr., 5.9.44

Antwortschreiben bitte Tagebuch - Nummer angeben

Geheime Reichssache !

F e r n s c h r e i b e n
=================================

An

ſſ-Standartenführer Ministerialrat Dr. B r a n d t
Persönlicher Stab Reichsführerſſ,
B e r l i n
============

Betr.: Jüdische Skelettsammlung

Gemäss Vorschlag vom 9.2.42 und dortiger Zustimmung vom 23.2.42
AR/493/37 wurde durch ſſ-Sturmbannführer Professor Hirt die
bisher fehlende Skelettsammlung angelegt. Infolge Umfang der
damit verbundenen wissenschaftlichen Arbeit sind Skelettierungs-
arbeiten noch nicht abgeschlossen. Hirt erbittet im Hinblick
auf etwa erforderlichen Zeitaufwand für 80 Stück Weisungen,
falls mit Bedrohung Strassburgs zu rechnen ist, wegen der Behandlung der im Leichenkeller der Anatomie befindlichen Sammlung.
Er kann Entfleischung und damit Unkenntlichmachung vornehmen,
dann allerdings Gesamtarbeit teilweise umsonst und grosser wissen-
schaftlicher Verlust für diese einzigartige Sammlung, weil da-
nach Hominitabgüsse nicht mehr möglich wären. Skelettsammlung als
solche nicht auffällig. Weichteile würden deklariert als bei
Übernahme Anatomie durch Franzosen hinterlassene alte Leichen-
reste und zur Verbrennung gegeben. Erbitte Entscheidung zu
folgenden Vorschlägen:

    1.) Sammlung kann erhalten bleiben
    2.) Sammlung ist teilweise aufzulösen
    3.) Sammlung ist im Ganzen aufzulösen.

(Sievers)

ſſ-Standartenführer

**Telegram of September 5, 1944 from Sievers to Brandt requesting
a decision as to what should be done with the collection of skeletons
prepared by Hirt in Strasbourg, in connection with the approach of
the Allied armies to the city.** (APMA-B, D-AuI-5/14, p. 237).

Translation:

TELEGRAM

To SS-Standartenführer Ministerial Counselor Dr. Brandt
Personal Staff of the Reichsführer
Berlin

Re: Collection of Jewish skeletons

In accordance with the proposal of 9.2.1942 and permission AR/493/37 therein granted as of 23.2.1942, SS-Sturmbannführer Prof. Hirt began a collection of skeletons, the lack of which had previously been felt acutely. In connection with the scope of this undertaking, the scientific work connected with the preparation of the skeletons has not yet been completed. In view of the investment of time required for 80 pieces, Hirt has made a request for instructions–in case Strasbourg is endangered–in respect to the further fate of the collection, located in the basement of the department of anatomy. He can perform the removal from the skeletons of the soft tissue and carry out procedures leading as a result to the remains becoming unrecognizable, although this would be accompanied by the partial loss to the overall project of the scientific value of this unique collection, since it would no longer be possible at a later date to make casts of the human bodies. The collection of skeletons itself is not something that attracts attention. The soft tissue, as is known, can be classified as old fragments of remains left over after the acquisition of the department of anatomy from the French and designated for cremation. You are asked to make a decision in reference to the following proposals:
  the collection to be secured in the appropriate way
  the collection to be partially liquidated
  the collection to be totally liquidated.

[signed]
Sievers
SS-Standartenführer

Excerpt from an article by Stanisław Kłodziński, former prisoner number 20019, on the collection of skeletons for the Reich University in Strasbourg.

Only after the war did Josef Kramer, the commandant of Natzweiler concentration camp, tried before the Military Tribunal in Strasbourg in 1945, reveal the subsequent fate of the victims [the Auschwitz prisoners picked for Hirt's skeleton collection]. (…)

The questioning of Kramer over the murder of the people chosen for the anatomy department in Strasbourg went as follows:

"I was a bookkeeper in Augsburg until 1932.Then I volunteered for the SS and was ordered to supervise concentration camp prisoners. Before the end of enemy activity, I was an officer in various concentration camps. (…) August 1943, I received orders from the camp in Oranienburg, or perhaps from an even higher SS command center in Berlin, to accept approximately 80 prisoners from Auschwitz. The letter accompanying that order instructed me to contact Professor Hirt from the medical school in Strasbourg immediately. I traveled to the anatomy Institute in Strasbourg, where Hirt informed me that he already knew about the arrival of the prisoners from Auschwitz in Struthof (Struthof was the old name of the Natzweiler camp). He also told me that these people should be killed with lethal gas in the gas chamber at the Struthof camp, and that their corpses should then be transferred to the anatomy institute, so that they would be at his disposal. After that, he gave me a bottle containing about 0.25 liters of salts, I think, of hydrogen cyanide salts. The professor told me more or less what dose I should use to poison the prisoners who would be arriving from Auschwitz. (…) At the beginning of August 1943, I obtained the 80 prisoners who were supposed to be poisoned with the gas I obtained from Hirt.

One evening, I arrived for the first time in a small truck at the gas chamber, taking 15 women with me. (…) I told those women that they were going to the disinfection chamber, but I did not tell them that they were going to be poisoned. With the help of several SS men, I stripped them naked, and, when they were naked, I pushed them into the gas chamber. (…) The next day, I ordered SS orderlies to place the corpses in the truck and take them to the institute of anatomy, as Dr. Hirt had instructed me. (…) Several days later, under the same circumstances, I again took a certain number of women to the gas chamber, where they were gassed in the same way. I went to the gas chamber again several days later and that was repeated 2 or 3 times, until I had killed 50 or perhaps 55 men with the salt given to me by Hirt."

On December 18, 1946, a French citizen, Henryk Henrypierre (…) testified before the Tribunal as follows: "In June 1942. (…) he applied for work in Strasbourg and was hired as a preparer in the institute of anatomy then directed by Prof. Hirt. One June day in 1943, Prof. Hirt directed him to prepare basins for 120 corpses. The first contingent consisted of 30 women's corpses that were still warm. Henrypierre wrote down on a piece of paper the tattooed numbers that were visible on the left forearms of the women. The corpses of 30 men arrived next, followed by the corpses of 27 more men. The corpses were conserved. After the arrival of the Allied armies in Strasbourg, Prof. Hirt ordered those corpses to be cut up into pieces and burned in the municipal crematorium."

Source: Stanisław Kłodziński, *Zbiór szkieletów żydowskich dla uniwersytetu III Rzeszy w Strasburgu*, "Przegląd Lekarski", 1 (1964), pp. 96–100.

Kurt Heissmeyer

Kurt Heissmeyer was born into a district doctor's family in Lammspringe in 1905. He studied medicine at various German universities. In 1933, he took a job as a doctor specializing in internal and lung diseases at the August-Viktor hospital in Hohenlychen, which came under the control of the SS in 1942.

He was a fanatical proponent of the National Socialist ideology, which he grafted onto his clinical practice and expressed in pseudoscientific, racist publications. While working on his habilitation [post-doctoral academic qualification] on the subject of preventing tuberculosis by infecting patients with tuberculosis of the skin in order to enhance their immunity, he obtained permission from the SS to experiment on concentration camp prisoners. Oswald Pohl directed him to the Neungamme camp for these experiments. He began his first trials on prisoners in June 1944, and carried out his final experiments on children in March 1945.

Dr. Kurt Heissmeyer's name featured on a list of war criminals in 1945, but only in 1963 was he arrested in Magdeburg. After an investigation lasting 2 years and a half, he was sentenced to life imprisonment, the loss of his honors and public rights, and the cost of the court proceedings. He died in prison in 1967[36].

---

[36] The following have written extensively on Kurt Heissmeyer's experiments: *Fritz Bringmann, Kindermord am Bullenhuser Damm. SS* – Verbrechen in Hamburg 1945: Menschenversuche an Kindern. Frankfurt am Mein 1978; Günther Schwarberg, *Der SS – Arzt und die Kinder. Bericht über den Mord vom Bullenhauser Damm*, Hamburg 1979.

Photographs of Jewish children transferred from Auschwitz to Neu-engamme Concentration Camp on November 27, 1944 for experimental purposes and subsequently murdered in the basement of the Bullenhauser Damm school in Hamburg on April 20, 1945.

Jaquelin Morgenstern, a Jewish girl from France, born May 26, 1932, lived with her parents in Paris.

The French police arrested the whole family and sent them to the collection camp in Drancy. They were deported to Auschwitz on May 20, 1944, and imprisoned in Birkenau after selection: Jaquelin and her mother in the women's camp, and her father in the men's camp. A short time later, her mother died and Jaquelin was transferred to the children's barracks. She was sent to Neuengamme on November 27, 1944. The photograph was taken in Paris when Jaquelin was 7.

Reproduced from a photograph provided by KZ Gedenkstätte Neuengamme

Ruchla Zylberberg, a Jewish girl born in the vicinity of Sandomierz, Poland, on May 6, 1936. Deported to Auschwitz with her mother and younger sister, both of whom died there. Ruchla was transferred to Neuengamme on November 27, 1944. The photograph was taken just before the German occupation of Poland.

Reproduced from a photograph provided by KZ Gedenkstätte Neuengamme.

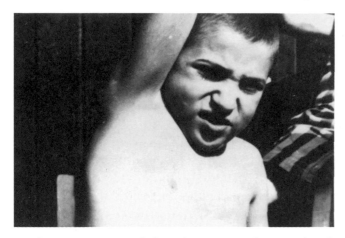

Mark James, a Jewish boy born in Radom, Poland, on March 17, 1939 and deported to Auschwitz in late July 1944. His transport was not subjected to selection on the Birkenau unloading ramp. Mark was designated as number B-1159 and placed n Birkenau along with his mother. He was sent to Neuengamme on November 27, 1944. Photograph taken in Neuengamme Concentration Camp.

Reproduced from a photograph provided by KZ Gedenkstätte Neuengamme.

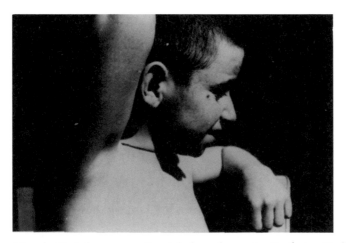

Marek Steinbaum, a Jewish boy born in Radom, Poland in 1934. Probably deported to Auschwitz with his parents in August 1944. After arriving at the unloading ramp, the Steinbaum family was sent to the camp. Marek's parents survived. Marek was sent to Neuengamme on November 27, 1944. He was hanged at a school in Hamburg at the age of 10. Photograph taken in Neuengamme Concentration Camp.

Reproduced from a photograph provided by KZ Gedenkstätte Neuengamme.

Excerpt from an article by Stanisław Sterkowicz, former Neuengamme concentration camp prisoner number 78536, on the pseudo-medical experiments conducted there by Dr. Kurt Heissmeyer.

In the fall of 1944, Heissmeyer wished to carry out suitable tuberculosis experiments on children. With the help of his protectors, Gebhart and Pohl, 20 Jewish children between the ages of 4 and 12 were brought specially from Auschwitz. These were Jewish children from various European countries, the majority of them from Poland. Heissmeyer carried out his cruel experiments on these children until March 1945. Within three months of the beginning of the experiments, tubercular changes appeared in the mid-thoracic nodes of the majority of the children. After four months there was infiltration, and tubercular lesions were observed in April 1945. On the basis of the collected documentation it was established that Dr. Kurt Heissmeyer performed experiments on about one hundred adults and twenty children in the course of his 9 months at Neuengamme.

Few people survived these experiments. Even those who managed to come through these criminal experiments were put to death at the hands of the Nazi thugs. This was the fate that awaited all the children subjected to the experiments. In the second half of April 1945, when it was plain to all Germans that nothing could save Nazi Germany, hasty efforts began to remove all evidence of the cruel experiments. Heissmeyer took the documentation of his research and concealed it in a special crate, and ordered it to be buried on the grounds of the hospital in Hohenlychen. As for the children, the living witnesses of Heissmeyer's "scientific work," the commandant of the Neuengamme camp, Obersturmbannführer SS Max Pauly, received orders by telephone from his superiors in Berlin to put them to death.

This order was carried out on the night of April 20/21, 1945. All the children, along with Dutch nurses and French prisoner doctors, were taken to a branch of the camp at a former school on Bullenhuserdamm in Hamburg. The children were accompanied by the camp physician, Albert Trzebinsky, who was responsible for carrying out the execution. SS Hauptsturmführer Arnold Strippel gave the direct order to kill the children by hanging.

The children were taken to a bomb shelter in the cellar of the school. They were ordered to undress there, and Dr. Trzebinsky injected them with morphine in order to put them to sleep or drug them. In turn, SS Unterscharführer Johann Frahm hanged the children from hooks attached to the central heating pipes. Their guardians, the Dutch nurses Deutekom and Hölzl, and the Frenchmen, the biologist Professor Florence and the x-ray technician Réné Quenouille, were hanged at the same time in a different room in the cellar. (…)

In the opinion of the expert witnesses, professors Prokop, Steinbruck, Schubert, and Landman, the experiments planned by Heissmeyer were pointless from the start. On the basis of the scientific literature accessible and certainly familiar to him, Heissmeyer must have known that tuberculosis cannot be treated by the method he used. What is more, Heissmeyer must have been aware that, where tuberculosis is already present, it is especially dangerous to induce a deliberate further infection. These trials were extremely dangerous, especially in reference to children who were highly susceptible to infection with tuberculosis.

Source: Stanisław Sterkowicz, *Pseudomedyczne eksperymenty w obozie Neuengamme*, "Przegląd Lekarski", 1 (1977), pp. 13–137.

Excerpt from an article by Stanisław Kłodziński, former Auschwitz prisoner no. 20019, on the criminal tuberculosis experiments at Neuengamme.

Following his hypothesis, Heissmeyer carried out similar procedures on children. He already knew from his own experience that these procedures were harmful to health. In the autumn of 1944, through Dr. Gebhard, he requested from Pohl the sending of 20 children to the camp in Neuengamme, as a result of which this number of children, of both sexes and between the ages of 5 and 12, arrived from Auschwitz around December 1944. As he requested, they were well fed and in good general condition. These were Jewish children, mostly from Poland, and free of tuberculosis. (…) In the period from the end of 1944 to March 1945, Heissmeyer repeated on the children all the procedures described in relation to adults. Extant photographs show clearly that, after subcutaneous injections of Koch bacilli, these children developed large tubercular sores. The lymph glands of most of the children were also removed surgically for further study. Heissmeyer's notes indicate that all 20 children were infected with virulent Koch bacilli, and that probes were inserted into the lungs of at least three of the children. The extant radiological images of the lungs of 7-year-old Desmonika, 12-year-old Morgenstern, and 12-year-old Birnbaum exhibit signs of sickness identical to those in the adults upon whom Heissmeyer experimented previously. After the procedures, the children had high fevers, lost their appetites, and became bedridden. In April 1945, after the procedures, one of the French boys was already dying. The children were so feeble that they had to be carried to be examined.

Source: Stanisław Kłodziński, *Zbrodnicze doświadczenia z zakresu gruźlicy w Neuengamme. Działalność Kurta Heissmeyera*, "Przegląd Lekarski", 1 (1969), pp. 86–91.

Excerpt from memoirs by Dr. Paulina Trocka, former prisoner number A-24156, who was assigned to accompany children sent from Auschwitz to Neuengamme Concentration Camp on November 27, 1944 for experimental purposes.

The camp commandant summoned me one day and told me that I must travel as a companion with a transport of children. Three nurses, one of them a laboratory assistant from Hungary, traveled with me. There were 10 boys and 10 girls aged 6 to 12, all of them Jews from different countries; two came from Paris. I asked why these children were being transported. I was told: all of them are children without families. I learned from the children that many of their families had been sent to labor camps.

An SS man escorted the transport consisting of 20 children, a doctor, and three nurses. They were placed in a special car added to a normal train, and thus looked normal to outside observers. During the journey, we had to remove all Jewish insignia in order to avoid attracting people's attention. In order to prevent people approaching us, they were told that it was a transport of people with typhus.

One of the children was from Paris, the 12-year-old son of Dr. Cohen who, as far as I remember, was the director of the Rothschild Hospital in Paris. When that boy saw Berlin from the train, he said, "If I knew an address, I would escape from here." (…)

Supplies for the trip were provided, consisting of chocolate and milk. After two days, we arrived at the Neuengamme camp at 10:00 at night. It was a camp for political prisoners, with no Jews. (…)

I saw someone weeping when they saw the children. (…).

I never saw the children again.(…)

After the war, after liberation, I read in a Belgian newspaper about the trial in Germany known as the "Nuremberg trial." (…) Mention was made there of a doctor and 20 children, about the doctor murdering 20 children, and a French doctor testified as a witness in this matter. It was said that biological experiments were conducted on the children with tuberculosis, and that this was a group of 20 children including two from Paris. The doctor killed them in the cellar.

The parents who knew that I accompanied the children had questions for me. Despite the presentation during the trial of the affair of a group of children, including two from Paris–I had no doubt that they were talking about my group–I did not say anything at first..

Source: APMA-B, Memoirs Collection, vol. 232, pp. 60–63.

Other Experiments

Excerpt from testimony by former prisoner doctor Jan Céspiva, a resident at the gynecology clinic in Prague, on the deliberate infection of pregnant women with typhus.

Another experiment that was carried out, Gypsy mothers who were due to give birth in a couple of days were deliberately infected with typhus in order to discover whether the placenta acted as a barrier against infection, in which case the child would be born healthy, or was not a barrier, in which case the child, too, would be infected with typhus. I was present when all these women gave birth. They gave birth with 40-degree [104 degrees Fahrenheit] fevers, in unsatisfactory hygienic conditions. I asked for soap so that I could wash my hands before delivery, and begged for an antiseptic, but the reply was that they would die regardless, and there was no difference between death by infection and any other [kind of death].

Blood was drawn from the arteries on the children's temples. (…)When the blood was drawn from the brain because of the doctor's inexperience, the child died. The blood was taken to be tested at a special bacteriological institute in Oświęcim. (…) These experiments were carried out 86 times. All of these women and children were killed, and some 20 of them were put to death by injections of phenol to the heart, and the strongest ones, who survived and recovered from the typhus to the point where they could walk, were taken in the end to the gas chambers. That happened in crematorium no. 2 in July 1943.

Source: APMA-B, Höss Trial Collection, vol. 28, pp. 34–35.

Excerpt from the memoirs of Dr. Rudolf Diem, former prisoner number 10022, referring to the experiments conducted by Drs. Herbert Wuttke[37] and Oskar Dienstbach.[38]

The first doctor I encountered in the camp hospital was SS physician Wuttke [in the original: **Wothke** – I. S.], whose first name I do not recall. I was then a nurse-doctor at the ward for patients suffering from the spinal meningitis that was then going around. The death rate among these patients was almost 100 percent. SS Dr. Wuttke was carrying out trials at that time of a specific that was then unknown to us and only later was revealed to be sulfanilamid. This doctor's method was as follows: after inserting a needle into the spinal canal, he extracted cerebrospinal fluid until the patient began screaming because of the pain in his head and convulsing. (…)He replaced the extracted fluid by injecting sulfanilamid into the canal, usually in even greater amounts, until the moment when the patient again began screaming from the pain in his head. After being treated according to this method, the patients usually died. SS Dr. Wuttke did not know how to perform a spinal tap; he grew irritated, hit the patients over the head so that they would bend over more, usually hit bone, and then called out for someone to give him a hammer so that he could penetrate to the canal. He excused his incompetence in these sorts of procedures by stating that it was impossible to penetrate to the canal because it had been thickened as a result of the meningitis inflammation. He therefore brought healthy prisoners in from the camp and tried to tap their spinal canals. Here too, when he managed to introduce the needle into the spinal canal, he extracted large quantities of fluid and then introduced pure sulfanilamid into the spinal canal in order to find out whether the symptoms of spinal meningitis would appear. Since the conditions were not aseptic, these healthy subjects also usually went on to develop spinal meningitis. In many cases, to make things worse, the victims of this sort of experiment had to go to their normal occupations in the camp and this doctor did not concern himself with their fate. (…)Wanting to find out whether or not the microorganism responsible for the widespread infection with spinal meningitis, as collected from the spinal canals of patients suffering from this illness, could induce the illness when injected in spinal fluid into a healthy spinal canal, he injected healthy prisoners with the infected material. It goes without saying that he induced the illness and the regrettable consequences of this experiment.

Oskar Dienstbach (…) was a specialist in piercing every body cavity: the thorax, abdomen, lungs, swollen joints, sinuses. He searched for exuda-

---

[37] Herbert Wuttke, born June 11, 1905 in Juliusberg, SS camp physician in Oświęcim 1940–1941.

[38] Oskar Dienstbach, SS-Standortarzt from the autumn of 1941 to March 2, 1942.

tions everywhere. (…) He did so brutally, drilling with a puncture needle into the lung in every direction with rotational motions. As a result of these examinations, the subjects very frequently hemorrhaged as a result of the rupture of blood vessels, and died.

Source: APMA-B, Memoirs Collection vol. 172, p. 136.

Excerpt from a deposition submitted during the trial of Rudolf Höss by Dr. Jan Grabczyński, former prisoner number 83846, employed in the Auschwitz camp hospital (block no. 21 of the main camp).

The SS doctors were under orders to receive some surgical training. It was assumed that each of them would know how to perform certain surgical procedures such as amputation, appendicitis, or hernia. (...) The doctors who trained there were: Entress, Lukas, Rhode, Thilo, Fischer, and König. They took no account at all of their surgical patients, and it was striking–abstracting from the human approach–that Entress was capable of operating on a patient one day and then, three days later, sending that patient to death by gassing or by a phenol injection. These German doctors had an exceptionally low level of education and knowledge.

Source: APMA-B, Höss Trial Collection, vol. 27, p. 14.

Annexes

Biographical Sketches of the Authors of Memoirs, Accounts, and Testimonies

AJDELMAN, EUGENIA – camp number A 13864.
Born in Lubartów, Poland, on February 23, 1924. Confined in the ghetto in Bełżyce near Lublin in December 1941, before being sent to the labor camp in Poniatowa, and then to Lublin Concentration Camp (Majdanek). She was secretly married while in the camp. Deported to Auschwitz in August 1944. She was pregnant at the time. Assigned to the road-roller labor detail, she quickly fell ill and was admitted to the camp hospital, where she was designated for abortion experiments. With the Red Army approaching and the camp evacuation underway, she managed to give birth. Her child died several days later as a result of the prevailing conditions. She was liberated in Auschwitz on January 27, 1945.

AKUNIS, DORA – camp number 38782.
Deported from Thessaloniki to Auschwitz in March 1943. Subjected to medical experimentation in the camp.

BARDIJ, TOMASZ – camp number unknown.
Born in Budapest in 1923. Deported to Auschwitz in a transport of Hungarian Jews in June 1944. Subjected to medical experiments here. He was liberated in Auschwitz on January 27, 1945.

BAROUCH, ALISA – camp number 41544.
Born in Thessaloniki on May 10, 1927. Deported to Auschwitz on April 17, 1943. Subjected to medical experiments.

BIAŁOSTOCKA, ALINA (in Auschwitz under the name BREWDA) – camp number 62761.
Born July 28, 1913, Warsaw. Transferred on orders from Dr. Lolling, head of Office DIII in the SS-WVHA, from Majdanek (Lublin Concentration Camp) to Auschwitz as a surgeon gynecologist on September 21, 1943. Named head physician of block no. 10, the experimental block in the Auschwitz main camp, with the status of block supervisor, in February 1944, giving

her access to all the records in the block. Removed from block no. 10 for "betrayal of secrets" and imprisoned in the "bunker" in July 1944. Transferred to Birkenau two weeks later. Restored to post of physician in January 1945. Evacuated to Neustadt Glewe Concentration Camp on January 18, 1945.

ČESPIVA, JAN – camp number 94638.
Doctor. Deported to Auschwitz from Bohemia on January 25, 1943. In Auschwitz until the end of August 1943, employed in the camp hospital.

DIEM, RUDOLF – camp number 10022.
Born in Hermanów on August 23, 1896. Polish Army doctor with the rank of major. Head of the sanitary service during the defense of Warsaw in the September 1939 campaign, he played an active role in clandestine work after the capitulation, including the supply of medicine and bandages to inmates in Pawiak prison.
Deported to Auschwitz on February 1, 1941. Employed as a prisoner doctor in the outpatient clinic in block no. 28 in the main camp, and later in the "hospital" in the Gypsy camp in Birkenau (sector BIIe). An active member of the resistance movement in the camp, he was in contact with Witold Pilecki. Liberated at Auschwitz on January 27, 1945.

FEJKIEL, WŁADYSŁAW – camp number 5647.
Doctor. He was born in Krościenko on January 1, 1911. After being deported to Auschwitz on October 8, 1940, he worked in various labor details before being employed in the prison hospital, where his jobs ranged from night watchman to senior prisoner. He was a member of the camp resistance movement. Liberated in Auschwitz on January 27, 1945. After the war, he was a professor at the Medical Academy in Cracow. He published a series of articles in *Przegląd Lekarski-Oświęcim* on the criminal medical experiments that Nazi doctors inflicted on Auschwitz prisoners; he died in 1995.

FIDERKIEWICZ, ALFRED — camp number 138907. Doctor. He was born in Horedenko in the Ukraine on July 2, 1886. A PPR [Polish Workers' Party, the communist party in Poland from 1942–1948-trans.] activist, he was arrested on June 28, 1943 and deported to Auschwitz on August 25, 1943 from Pawiak prison in Warsaw. He continued his resistance work in Auschwitz, mostly through helping fellow prisoners. Employed in the camp "hospital" as a doctor, he was liberated from Auschwitz on January 27, 1945. After the war, he was briefly mayor of Cracow.

Next, he became director of the Main Commission for the Investigation of Nazi Crimes in Poland. He worked in the diplomatic service and was active in the Health Services Labor Union. He wrote several books, mainly memoirs, including *Brzezinka. Wspomnienia z obozu.*

FLECHNER, ALBERT – camp number 65566.

(Jew from France) doctor, born 1917. Deported to Auschwitz in September 1942 in a mass transport from the camp at Drancy. He did various kinds of work on the grounds of the camp for the first few months. When he fell ill he was sent to the camp hospital and, after recovering thanks to care by prisoner doctors, he was employed there first as an orderly and later as a physician. Liberated in Auschwitz on January 27, 1945.

FREJDIN, ŻAK – camp number B 3759.

Born in Paris on January 11, 1914. Deported to Auschwitz on August 4, 1944. Subjected to medical experimentation in the camp. He was liberated in Auschwitz on January 27, 1945.

GŁOWA, STANISŁAW – camp number 20017. Born in Igołomia on September 15, 1898. Fought in the defensive war in September 1939. Arrested in June 1941 and sent to Auschwitz on August 12. Assigned to the mowers' labor detail and later worked on flood control on the river Soła. Fell ill in October 1941 and admitted to the camp hospital. When his health improved, he became a ward attendant in block no. 20. Soon afterwards, he began working as a nurse's aid, and then a nurse. Became the scribe in block no. 20; held that post until August 1944. Active in the illegal supply of medication to the camp and collecting evidence of the crimes committed in Auschwitz; made clandestine copies of hospital documents. This documentation was later smuggled out of the camp. One of 60 prisoners jailed in the basement of block no. 11 on August 15, 1944, on charges of resistance movement activity. Finally transferred to the Sachsenhausen Concentration Camp on August 30, 1944; liberated in Germany on May 3, 1945. Testified after the war at the trial of Rudolf Höss.

GOTTLIEBOVA, (BABBITT) DINAH – camp number 61016.
Painter, born in Brno on January 21, 1923; enrolled in the Umělecké Průmyslovke there. Deported, with her mother, to the Theresienstadt ghetto-camp on January 28, 1942, and transported from there to Auschwitz on September 8, 1943. Imprisoned in the so-called Famielienlager Theresienstadt (the family camp in Birkenau sector BIIb), she first painted numbers on the buildings. She did several wall paintings of Disney scenes on the walls inside the children's barracks. This caught the attention of SS camp doctor Lukas, and later of Dr. Mengele, on whose orders she painted portraits of Gypsies from various countries in 1944, and also of prisoners suffering from noma. On January 1, 1945, she was transferred to Ravensbrück Concentration Camp, and later to the Neustadt-Glewe sub-camp, where she was liberated on May 2, 1945. After the war, she went first to Paris and later to the USA. She never returned to Auschwitz themes in her painting, and had her tattooed camp number removed. Several of her portraits of Gypsies are in the collections of the Auschwitz-Birkenau State Museum.

GRABCZYŃSKI, JAN – camp number 83864.
Surgeon, born in Tarnów on August 21, 1908. Deported to Auschwitz on December 16, 1942 and assigned to work in the camp "hospital" in block no. 21. Starting as a helper, he became a nurse, surgeon, and finally, in 1944, head of the surgical department. Thanks to the efforts of his family, Dr. Grabczyński was "released" from the camp on March 30, 1944, but was nevertheless forced, because he was highly qualified, to remain in Auschwitz as a "*Zivilarbeiter*" (civilian worker) at the service of a camp physician Eduard Wirths. Grabczyński escaped in August 1944 and remained in hiding in Cracow until the end of the war. After liberation, he helped set up the Polish Red Cross hospital that aided sick prisoners at the site of the camp.

GROSMAN, MAKSIM – camp number A-5419.
(Jew from Yugoslavia), doctor, born 1893. Emigrated from Yugoslavia to Italy with his family in 1941. In 1943, his wife and two children went to Switzerland, but he had to remain in Italy because he was ill. He was arrested by the Germans in March 1944 and deported to Auschwitz in May. He was employed as a doctor in the camp hospital. Liberated in Auschwitz on January 27, 1945.

HALSKA, MARIA (known in the camp as Maria Hanel) – camp number 38396.
Born in Tomaszów Mazowiecki on February 20, 1903. Dentist. Arrested in a roundup at the train station in Cracow on March 15, 1943 and imprisoned in Auschwitz. She was the successor at the *Zahnstation* (dentist's office) in Birkenau of the head dentist, the French communist activist Danielle Casanova, who contracted typhus and died soon afterward. Barrack no. 30 in sector BIa, where she was in charge of the dentist's office, became under her administration a place of recuperation for exhausted prisoners who, while „waiting" to be seen, had a chance to marshal their strength for a few more days of life in the camp. Maria Mandel caught Halska „organizing" [illegally acquiring] food and punished her by sending her to the penal company, where Halska had to dig ditches. After release from this penal labor detail and a talk with Dr. Mengele, Halska was employed carrying out research on dental anomalies in twins. After leaving Auschwitz in the Death March she was transferred to Ravensbrück Concentration Camp, and later to the labor camp in Malhof, where she held the post of dentist. On April 26, 1945, the local Red Cross evacuated her to Sweden. In her new surroundings she continued her professional practice on the strength of a dental license granted to her personally by King Gustav V. Later in the 1940s she returned to Poland and settled in Warsaw. She was a dentist for members of ZBoWiD [the official veterans' organization] and also a member of the ZBoWiD board of directors.

HARPMAN, MITIE – camp number 62493.
Born in Amsterdam on December 27, 1902. Deported to Auschwitz on September 15, 1943. Subjected to medical experimentation in the camp.

KĘPA, STEFAN – camp number 799.
Born in Gidly near Radomsko on July 15, 1909. Bookkeeper. Arrested March 27, 1940, in the Nowy Sącz area for activity in a Polish underground organization including assisting Poles to escape through Slovakia to Hungary, in order to travel from there to France where Polish Army units were being formed. Kępa was sent to Auschwitz on June 20, 1940, in the second prisoner transport in the history of the camp and the first from Wiśnicz. Until the end of 1940 he worked in the Rollwagenkommando. In early winter he managed to transfer to the camp metalworkers' workshop despite having no familiarity with the trade. In June 1941, as punishment for „organizing" [illegally acquiring] potatoes, he was sent to the Buna-Werke labor detail, where he worked laying railroad tracks. Later he was assigned to the Kiesgrube labor commando, which toiled in the gravel pit. In July 1942, he was placed in the Monowitz sub-camp, where he fell ill for the second time

with typhus. In the „hospital" at Monowice he was forced to swallow experimental pills and pellets. After recuperating thanks to the help of other prisoners, he returned to the metalworkers' workshop in the main camp, this time as bookkeeper. He secretly kept notes on the SS men, capos, and other prisoner functionaries, and buried these notes before departing from the camp on October 29, 1944. He was sent for a short time to Sachsenhausen concentration camp, and then to Buchenwald where he remained until liberation. In 1946, he traveled to the site of the Auschwitz camp and dug up his notes, which served as valuable evidence in the trials of SS men from the Auschwitz Concentration Camp SS garrison.

KIETA, MIECZYSŁAW – camp number 59590.
Born in Cracow on December 30, 1920. Journalist. Deported to Auschwitz on August 17, 1942. After various other labor assignments, he was sent to the Hygiene Institute in Rajsko in early 1943 because of his command of German and typing skills. His main task was keeping a running inventory of the apparatus and other equipment at the laboratory. Transferred to the Gross-Rosen Concentration Camp on November 19, 1944, and later to the Leitmeritz sub-camp of Flossenbürg Concentration Camp.

KLEIN, OTTO – camp number A 5332.
Born June 7, 1932. Deported to Auschwitz on June 27, 1944. During selection on the unloading ramp, he and his twin brother were picked for Dr. Mengele's experiments. He was liberated in Auschwitz on January 27, 1945.

KŁODZIŃSKI, STANISŁAW – camp number 20019.
Born in Cracow on May 4, 1918; had completed three years of medical school at the Jagiellonian University when World War II broke out. Volunteered to serve in a hospital in Cracow, and worked for the RGO (Main Welfare Board). He joined the underground, using the code-name "Stakło." Arrested on June 18, 1941, he spent 2 months under investigative custody in Montelupich prison. Deported to Auschwitz on August 12, 1941, and joined the camp resistance movement. The organization's contacts with the outside world enabled him to obtain drugs and bandages, mostly intended for sick prisoners. From January 1942, he worked as an orderly in the camp hospital in block no. 20 of the main camp. Evacuated to Mauthausen Concentration Camp on January 18, 1945, and liberated there on May 5. He cared for his fellow prisoners there until July 12, and then returned to Poland. After finishing

medical school, he took a post in the Tuberculosis Clinic at the Academy of Medicine in Cracow. He published over 300 articles on tuberculosis, the epidemiology of contagious diseases, and the so-called KZ Syndrome (the medical, psychological, and sociological after-effects suffered by former concentration camp prisoners). He was a member of the Main Commission for the Investigation of Nazi Crimes in Poland, the Auschwitz Preservation Society, and the International Auschwitz Committee, and collaborated with the Auschwitz Museum. Published a series of articles in *Przegląd Lekarski -Oświęcim* on experiments conducted at Auschwitz Concentration Camp by German doctors as well as biographical profiles of prisoner doctors employed in the camp hospitals who risked their lives to help their fellow prisoners.

He died in Cracow in 1990.

KOPYT, TADEUSZ – number 2151.

Typesetter born in Opacza on August 25, 1920. Arrested during a street roundup in Warsaw on August 11, 1940; deported to Auschwitz on August 15, 1940, in the first Warsaw transport. Assigned to work in the *Landwirtschaft* labor detail, the camp printing press (briefly), the potato room, and the *Zerlegebetriebe* (aircraft salvage). While in Auschwitz, he was sent to the penal company on two different occasions: once for destroying paper in the camp printing press, and once for attempting to escape. Transferred to Gross-Rosen Concentration Camp in 1944, and evacuated from there to other camps in the depths of Germany in February 1945. Liberated by the US Army.

KULA, MICHAŁ – camp number 2718.

Born in Trzebinia, Poland, on September 7, 1912. Arrested in Warsaw on August 6, 1940, deported to Auschwitz on August 15. Assigned to the locksmith's workshop in the camp. Transferred to Mauthausen Concentration Camp in October 1944.

LORENCI, ANDREAS – camp number A 12090.
Born in Hungary on May 20, 1934. Deported to Auschwitz in May 1944. He and his twin sister were subjected to medical experiments. He was liberated in Auschwitz on January 27, 1945.

MARKOWSKI, STEFAN – camp number 64914.
Born June 17, 1911 in Maciejowice. Carpenter. Deported to Auschwitz from the prison in Lublin Castle on September 22, 1942. For the first two months he worked in the camp carpentry workshop, after which he was admitted to the hospital. The prisoner doctors there discharged him before an expected selection and he was assigned to the Leichenkommando –the corpse-carriers' labor detail. Initially, he carried corpses from the hospital blocks to the morgue located in the cellar of block no. 28, and from July 1943 to August 1944 he worked in a similar capacity in block no. 11, clearing the court yard after mass executions at the Death Wall. On October 25, 1944, he was transferred to Sachsenhausen Concentration Camp, where he remained until liberation.

MEC, ADOLF – camp number B-13877.
(Jew from Germany), doctor, born 1899. Deported to Auschwitz in October 1944. Employed as a doctor in the camp hospital. Liberated in Auschwitz on January 27, 1945.

MINC, KAREL – camp number 68582.
Born December 30, 1909 at Šternov in today's Czech Republic. Photographer. Arrested in 1939. Imprisoned in Dachau (six weeks) and Buchenwald concentration camps. Deported to Auschwitz on October 19, 1942 and assigned to construction work during the expansion of the Monowice sub-camp. Thanks to the fact that he knew one of the disinfectors, Dr. Hanak, he became the latter's assistant for corpse transportation. He miraculously avoided being sent to the gas chamber on several occasions. In order to spare him unnecessary stress, Ludwig Wörl (*Lagerältester* HKB in Monowice and a friends of Hanak's) employed Minc as a *Pfleger* (orderly) at the outpatient clinic in Monowice. On January 18, 1945, he set out on the Death March to Gliwice, before being taken from there by train to Buchenwald, where he was liberated.

MROCZKOWSKI, ZBIGNIEW – camp number 16840.
Engineer, born in Cracow on December 8, 1912. Arrested in Warsaw on February 11, 1941 and imprisoned in Pawiak; deported to Auschwitz on May 29, 1941. First assigned to labor in the Buna-Werke detail, on the construction of the artificial gasoline plant. Sent to the camp hospital after falling

ill in February 1942. After recovering, he began working in the Hygiene Institute in Rajsko, where he built laboratory apparatus and equipment for Dr. Weber. Transferred to the camp in Łagisza in May 1943. Escaped during the evacuation of the camp in January 1945.

NYISZLI, MIKLŇS – camp number A-8450.
Born in Somlyo, Romania, on July 17, 1901. He enrolled in medical school at Cluj (Kolozsvar) University in 1920. After his first year there, he transferred to Kiel University in Germany, before finally graduating in Breslau (now Wrocław) in 1930. Having received his MD degree, he returned to Romania. In 1937, he and his family moved to the small town of Viseu de Sus, which was transferred to Hungary as a result of the Romanian-Hungarian treaty of 1940. After the occupation of Hungary by the German army, Nyiszli and his family were deported to Auschwitz in the second half of May 1944. During selection on the ramp in Birkenau, Nyiszli, his wife, and his daughter were sent to the camp. Owing to his expertise in forensic medicine, Dr. Mengele employed him as a specialist to carry out autopsies on the corpses of twins and dwarves. He was quartered in a room at crematorium I (II) in Birkenau, and was a direct eyewitness to the extermination of the Jews in the gas chambers. Evacuated from Auschwitz in January 1945, he was liberated by the Americans at the Ebensee camp on May 5, 1945. After returning to Romania, he resumed work as a doctor. He testified at the IG Farbenindustrie trial in Nuremberg in October 1947. He died of a heart attack in 1956.

OLBRYCHT, JAN – camp number 46688.
Born May 6, 1886. Professor of medicine at the Jagiellonian University in Cracow, court-certified forensic expert. Member of the Polish Academy of Learned Sciences, French Forensic Medicine and Public Health Association, and International Academy of Forensic Medicine and Public Health. Arrested in Cracow on June 30, 1942, incarcerated in Montelupich prison there, and deported to Auschwitz on July 13. Served at first as a cleaner in block no. 11; came down with starvation diarrhea after several weeks and sent to the camp hospital. After recuperation, employed there to sort medicines supplied by the „Kanada" warehouses, and then appointed head of the pharmacy at the hospital for prisoners. As a member of the Polish intelligentsia, concealed his educational accomplishments for reasons of personal safety; when the truth came out, he began being employed as a pathologist by SS doctors. Evacuated from Auschwitz in the March of Death on January 18, 1945, and reached Mauthausen, where he remained until liberation.

PACZUŁA, TADEUSZ – camp number 7725.
Born in Gliwice on November 26, 1920. Medical student. Arrested December 18, 1940, in Nowy Bytom (today a district in Ruda Śląska) for activity in a Polish underground organization. Imprisoned in Auschwitz Concentration Camp that same day. Worked in the *Abbruchkommando*, demolishing houses in the village of Monowice, then on the construction of the Buna-Werke chemical plant, and from 1943 in the clerks' chamber (*Schreibstube*) of the camp hospital in the Auschwitz main plant. Released from the camp on September 27, 1944.

PLESZOWSKA, FELICJA – camp number 29875.
Born in Warsaw on July 28, 1913. Arrested at the end of December 1942 and incarcerated in Auschwitz on January 18, 1943. Initially employed at jobs connected with the expansion of the camp; later assigned as a medical instruments nurse to barrack no. 30 in the women's camp in Birkenau (sector BIa), and then to block no. 10, the experimentation block, in the main camp.

SCHICK, HANI – camp number A-7043.
Hungarian Jew, arrested in Szatmar together with her husband and three children (including a set of twins) on May 28, 1944, and deported to Auschwitz. The twins were subjected by Dr. Mengele to medical experiments as a result of which they died; Hani's third child, her son Otto, died several days after the liberation of the camp. Her husband also died. Hani survived the camp thanks to the help of Ena Weiss, head prisoner doctor of the camp hospital.

SKURNIK, JAKOB – camp number 80629.
Born in Szerba, Poland, in 1925. Deported to Auschwitz on November 21, 1942. Subjected to medical experimentation in the camp. Liberated in Auschwitz on January 27, 1945.

STAPF, ADAM – camp number 3704.
Arrested in Cracow in July 1940, and transported to Auschwitz on August 28. First assigned to labor at road building in Birkenau and then at the final construction work on crematorium no. I. In December 1940, assigned to work in the *Effektenkammer*, first cleaning and later as a helper in the storage areas. Briefly labored at the Buna-Werke construction site in September 1941. Admitted to the camp hospital for 6 weeks in December in a state of total exhaustion. After convalescing, he returned to work at the *Effektenkammer* and remained there (with a short break from January to April 1944, laboring in the "Kanada" detail) until July 30, 1944, when he was transferred to Ravensbrück, where he was liberated.

STOPPELMAN, MARIA – camp number 82325.
Born in Amsterdam on May 22, 1914. A Jew of Dutch origins. Medical doctor. Arrested in Wangeningen, Netherlands on May 20, 1944, on charges of membership in a clandestine organization. Deported to Auschwitz on June 30. Employed as a technician in the analytical laboratory at the hospital in the women's camp, where her superior was Dr. Josef Mengele. Evacuated in the Death March in January 1945.

SZARBEL, JÓZEF DAWID – camp number 83397.
Born in Zakroczyn on April 9, 1916. Deported from the ghetto in Nowy Dwór Mazowiecki to Auschwitz on December 14, 1942. First assigned to labor at landscaping tasks in Birkenau. Later sent to the so-called bricklayers' school (*Mauerschule*), where prisoners were taught to lay bricks in connection with the expansion of the camp. Subjected to sterilization experiments in July 1943. Transferred to the Janina-Grube sub-camp in Libiąż in September 1943, where he worked in the coal mine. Evacuated to Buchenwald in January 1945.

SZYMAŃSKA, DANUTA (in Auschwitz under the name MARKOWSKA) – camp number 43536.
Transported to Auschwitz from Warsaw on April 29, 1943. Sent to work in June 1943 at the hospital in the Gypsy family camp (sector BIIe), where she remained until the second half of June 1944. She worked first in block no. 26 and next in block no. 22 as a nurse. In August 1944, she was transported to Ravensbrück, and then to Sachsenhausen, where she was a slave laborer in the Siemens factory.

TONDOS, WŁADYSŁAW – camp number 18871.
Born in Kalina Mała near Miechów on October 6, 1900. After the September defeat, he became involved in clandestine activity, joining the ZWZ [Union of Armed Struggle] in 1940. Arrested in Zakopane, where he was subjected to an extremely brutal interrogation in the notorious "Palace," the local Gestapo headquarters. Before deportation to Auschwitz, he spent 6 weeks in Tarnów prison. After arriving in Auschwitz on July 29, 1941, he was employed in the prison hospital in block no. 20, where he cared primarily for tuberculosis sufferers. He saved many prisoners from death. Thanks to cooperation between the camp resistance movement and the clandestine organization in the local vicinity, he obtained the necessary medication for the treatment of tuberculosis. Many prisoners who met him in the camp recalled his great devotion and dedication to the patients. On August 25, 1944, he was transferred to the Neuengamme Concentration Camp, where he was liberated on April 29, 1945.

TOPÓR, KAZIMIERA – camp number 25923.
Born in Misztwa, Poland, on February 21, 1924. Arrested together with her mother in 1942 for clandestine activity and imprisoned in Auschwitz on November 25 of that year. Employed as a cleaning woman in barrack no. 30 in the Birkenau women's camp (sector BIa). In January 1943, she was deliberately infected with typhus for experimental purposes. Thanks to her sister's intervention , she was released in March 1943.

TROCKA, PAULINA – camp number A- 24156.
Dentist and doctor, born in Kishinev (now Chisinau, Moldova) on December 28, 1905. She moved to Belgium in 1923. Active in the resistance movement during the war. Arrested for political reasons and deported to Auschwitz in July 1944; employed as a doctor in the women's camp in Birkenau.
Accompanied a group of 20 Jewish children sent to the Neuengamme Concentration Camp on November 27, 1944 (the children were subjects of experiments by Dr. Kurt Heissmeyer).

After several weeks in Neuengamme, Dr. Trocka was sent to the camp in Berghof.

TUSZNIO, APOLONIA – camp number 63873.
Arrested for underground activity and deported to Auschwitz on October 2, 1943. After quarantine, she came down with typhus and was admitted to the hospital. Sentenced to death after multiple interrogations by the Gestapo. Subjected to sterilization experiments in block no. 10 in the Auschwitz main camp. Transferred some time later to Mitweiden, from where she escaped. Re-arrested and incarcerated in various prisons and Ravensbrück Concentration Camp.

WARSZAWSKA-PIEKUT, ELŻBIETA – code name "Jaskółka" – camp number 46506.
Born in Kalisz on November 22, 1920.
Arrested for belonging to the AK (Home Army). Sent in a transport from Cracow to Auschwitz on June 24, 1943. Assigned as nurse to a barracks housing women employed in external labor details, where she bandaged injuries they received while working, mostly as a result of beatings. Assigned in 1944 to be a nurse in a new block for Jewish twins experimented on by Dr. Josef Mengele. Transferred to Ravensbrück in January 1945, and later to Neustadt-Glewe, where she was liberated. Stayed on for several months at a hospital set up there; returned to Poland in September 1945.

WITEK STANISŁAW – camp number 9355.
Born in Cracow on March 9, 1916. Arrested for clandestine activity on March 24, 1940 and deported to Auschwitz in January 1941. Employed in the camp in various labor details: as a stoker, unloading shipments of building materials, and on the construction of the Buna chemical complex. Also spent time in the penal company. After recovering from typhus, employed

in the prisoner kitchen and later in the potato room. Aided other prisoners by supplying them with food. Evacuated to Sachsenhausen Concentration Camp in October 1944.

WŁODARSKI, ZBIGNIEW – camp number 150172.
Born in Ostrowiec Świętokrzyski on December 4, 1922. Member of the AK. Arrested in July 1943. Refused to admit to underground activity, despite savage torture. Transported to Auschwitz on September 14, 1943, and placed in quarantine in Birkenau (sector BIIa). Transferred at the end of September to the main camp after being told that he would be employed as a nurse; subjected to pharmacological experiments instead. After recovery, employed as an orderly at the outpatient clinic in Birkenau sector BIId.

WOLMAN, JAKUB – camp number 33 611.
Born in Poland on July 13, 1914. Deported to Auschwitz from Slovakia in April 1942. Employed in the camp first as a nurse and then as a prisoner physician in the main camp hospital (block no. 21). He was liberated in Auschwitz on January 27, 1945.

WOYCICKI, ALFRED – camp number 39247.
Born in Lwów on June 21, 1906. Worked for Polish Radio before the war. Arrested in Cracow on February 18, 1942, for belonging to the resistance movement. Transported to Auschwitz from Montelupich prison on June 11, 1942. Thanks to the good offices of fellow prisoners, assigned to a job in the Erkennungsdienst (the identification service of the political department). Starting out doing manual labor, he became the scribe of the labor detail, was put in charge of the office and the photographic archive, and helped in the laboratory. Involved in the camp resistance movement. After the camp Gestapo broke up Col. Juliusz Gilewicz's clandestine ZWZ/AK cell, Woycicki was jailed in block no. 11. He was one of the few members of the cell who avoided being shot at the Death Wall on October 11, 1943. Evacuated to Gross-Rosen Concentration Camp in 1944, and from there to other camps. Liberated at the Neuengamme sub-camp in Litomierzyce on May 8, 1945.

VOHRYZKOVA, ILONA – camp number 31496.

Czech Jew, born June 10, 1915. On December 5, 1942, she was deported to the Theresienstadt ghetto/camp, from where she was transported to Auschwitz Concentration Camp on January 23, 1943. She was a nurse in Dr. Carl Clausberg's experimentation unit, first in block no. 30 in the Birkenau women's camp (sector BIa) and later in block no. 10 in the main camp.

Glossary

Arbeitseinsatz – camp department for assigning prisoners to labor.

Aussenkomando – external labor details that worked outside the camp.

Bauleitung – Zentralbauleitung der Waffen SS und Polizei Auschwitz O/S (Central Construction Authority) – office in charge of construction at Auschwitz Concentration Camp.

Bauhof – fenced-off area near the railroad spur next to the main camp, used for storing construction material.

DAW – Deutsche Ausrüstungswerke (German Equipment Works) – SS company that used prisoners to produce ammunition crates, furniture, and woodwork; also had metalworking shops and added weaving shops and an aircraft salvage operation in 1943.

Durchfall – starvation diarrhea, during which bacterial infections impair the functioning of the digestive tract.

Effektenkammer – warehouse containing items seized from Auschwitz prisoners.

Erkennungsdienst – the identification service of the camp Gestapo, which took mug shots of prisoners and documented pseudomedical experiments by SS doctors.

FKL (Frauenkonzentrationslager) – women's concentration camp. The first transports of women arrived in Auschwitz on March 26, 1942. Ten blocks in the main camp were surrounded with a high wall of concrete panels to create the *Frauenabteilung* (women's division). As more transports arrived and the blocks became overcrowded, the camp authorities decided in August 1942 to transfer the women's camp to Birkenau sector BIa. Sector BIb was added to the women's camp in July 1943. Until July 1943, the office of the commandant of Ravensbrück Concentration Camp was in charge of the Auschwitz women's camp. At that point, the women's camp came under the direct authority of the commandant of Auschwitz Concentration Camp.

Häftling – prisoner.

HKB – Häftlingskrankenbau – hospital for prisoners.

IG Farben – Interessengemeinschaft Farbenindustrie A.G.–Syndicate of Dyestuff Corporations, Inc.–the largest German chemical company, with a dominant position in artificial rubber and fuel production.

Industriehof – a separate area near the Main Camp where barracks housed workshops and storage.

"Kanada" – camp warehouses for possessions plundered from the Jews deported to Auschwitz for extermination. This property was inspected, sorted, packed, and shipped for use buy various Nazi organizations, or sold to private German companies. Valuables such as gold, precious stones, and foreign currency were sent to the Main Economic-Administrative Office, and from there to the Reich Bank.

Kapo – capo, prisoner functionary, overseer of a prisoner labor detail.

Penal Company (*Strafkompanie*** – SK)** – prisoners were sent there for periods of from one month to one year as punishment for various minor offenses. The prisoners did hard labor while SS or prisoner functionary overseers harassed them. Assignment to the labor company was regarded as one of the harshest penalties in the camp.

Kommando – prisoner labor detail.

Quarantine – many prisoners spent a period of several days to several weeks in quarantine when they arrived. This period included deliberate harassment intended to intimidate the prisoners and train them to obey the SS and prisoner functionaries unquestioningly. The harassment included scrupulously following the daily schedule, hours of exercises known as "sport," and instruction in lining up on the roll call square. To a lesser degree, quarantine served to identify and isolate sick prisoners among the new arrivals.

Lagererweiterung – (*Schutzhaftlagererweiterung*) camp extension – additional blocks built near the main camp (Auschwitz I) to house prisoners and store property plundered from extermination victims. In the summer of 1944, it mainly held Jewish women from Hungary, who were arriving in such numbers that they could not be put through selection. They were housed in barracks without any utilities or furnishings–no lighting, water, or sewers. Several hundred women slept on the bare ground in each barracks. They were not entered in the camp records. Young, healthy women were taken away to work in armaments factories; those regarded as unfit for labor were put to death in the gas chambers.

Muzułman –"Muselmann"–prisoner in a state of extreme mental and physical exhaustion.

Union – Werke - (Weichsel Union Metallwerke) – an armaments firm evacuated from Zaporozhets in the Ukraine in October 1943, which produced fuses for artillery shells after taking over the machinery and equipment of the Krupp factory in Oświęcim.

Politische Abteilung – political department, the camp Gestapo. Headed from 1940 by SS officer Maksymilian Grabner, who was succeeded in December 1943 by Hans Schurz.

Revier – camp hospital (literally, infirmary).

Zugang – newly arrived prisoner.

Timeline of Important Events in Auschwitz Concentration Camp[39]

April 1940 – Heinrich Himmler ordered the founding of a concentration camp, which would be built and expanded by prisoner labor, in old army barracks in Oświęcim.

May 4, 1940 – Rudolf Höss is officially named commandant of Konzentrationslager Auschwitz.

June 14, 1940 – the first transport of Polish political prisoners arrives from the prison in Tarnów (728 men).

July 6, 1940 – Tadeusz Wiejowski, a Pole, is the first prisoner to escape. In reprisal, all prisoners are subjected to a 20-hour-long punitive roll call.

November 22, 1940 – the first executions by shooting (40 Polish prisoners).

March 1, 1941 – the first visit to Auschwitz by Heinrich Himmler, who orders that the camp be expanded to hold 30 thousand prisoners, that a new camp to hold 100 thousand POWs be built on the site of the village of Brzezinka, and that 10 thousand prisoners be supplied to the IG Farbenindustrie company for the construction of a plant in Monowice-Dwory on the outskirts of Oświęcim.

April 23, 1941 – for the first time, 10 hostages were sentenced to death by starvation in reprisal for an escape by a prisoner. During a selection in similar circumstances on July 28, 1941, the Polish Franciscan missionary priest Maksymilian Rajmund Kolbe stepped forward and asked to be included in the group marked for death in the place of one of the despairing men who was chosen. After surviving for two weeks, Father Maksymilian Kolbe was put to death by phenol injection.

April 1941 – Prisoners began work on the construction of the Buna-Werke, walking 7 kilometers to the building site each morning and 7 kilometers back after work.

July 28, 1941 – a special commission arrives in Auschwitz and selects 575 prisoners, mostly Poles, to die in the euthanasia program for the "incurably ill"; the commission sends them to Sonnenstein, where they are put to death with carbon monoxide.

September 3, 1941 – approximately 600 Soviet POWs and 250 prisoners selected in the camp hospital were put to death with Zyklon B in the cellars of block no. 11.

---

39 Based on Danuta Czech, *Kalendarza wydarzeń w KL Auschwitz* [Auschwitz Chronicle] (Oświęcim, 1992), pp. 14-862.

October 7, 1941 – the first mass transport of Soviet POWs arrived and was housed in 9 blocks fenced off to create the Russisches Kriegsgefangenen Arbeitslager (Russian POW labor camp).

November 11, 1941 – the first execution at the Death Wall in the courtyard of block no. 11. The condemned men were led singly to the wall, stripped naked and with their hands fettered behind their backs. The executions were performed by a point-blank shot to the nape of the neck with a small-caliber weapon.

1942 – a mass estermination of Jews in gas chmbers has begun.

March 1942 – the separate camp for Soviet POWs was liquidated. The approximately 900 POWs remaining alive, and some prisoners, were transferred to the camp in Brzezinka (Birkenau), which was still under construction.

March 26, 1942 – the first transports of women arrived: 999 prisoners from Ravensbrück and 999 Jewish women from Poprad, Slovakia. A separate women's division (Frauenabteilung), subordinated to the office of the commandant of Ravensbrück, was set up in blocks nos. 1-10.

April 1942 – the first provisional gas chamber in Birkenau, known as "bunker no. 1" or "the little red house," was set up in a specially adapted farmhouse. The bodies of the victims were buried in mass graves in a nearby meadow.

June 10, 1942 – mutiny by prisoners in the penal company. Nine prisoners escaped, 13 were shot while attempting to escape, 20 more were shot during roll call, and about 320 were murdered in the gas chambers.

July 4, 1942 – the beginning of regular selections of Jews arriving in RSHA transports.

July 17-18, 1942 – Himmler's second visit (he watched the selection of an arriving transport of Jews, killing by gas in bunker no. 2, and the "emptying of the bunker."

August 6, 1942 – start of the transfer of women prisoners from Auschwitz to Birkenau sector BIa.

September 1942 – the open-air burning of corpses exhumed from mass graves began in Birkenau; approximately 100,000 bodies burned in this way through the end of November.

October 26, 1942 – approximately 500 prisoners from the main camp were transferred to the newly opened sub-camp in the village of Monowice (from which civilians have been expelled), near where the IG Farbenindustrie factory is under construction. The sub-camp is named Buda and is a part of Auschwitz.

October 28, 1942 – the largest execution in the history of the camp. After morning roll call, approximately 280 prisoners were taken under heavy

SS guard to block no. 11 and shot there in reprisal for sabotage and partisan operations in the Lublin region.

February 26, 1943 – arrival of the first transport of Gypsy families. They were placed in Birkenau sector BIIe, which was named the *Zigeunerlager.*

March 22, 1943 – the first of four crematorium buildings with gas chambers went into operation in Birkenau.

July 19, 1943 – 12 Polish prisoners from the surveyors' detail were hanged in reprisal for the escape of three prisoners from the detail. A collective gallows was built in the square in front of the kitchen. The execution was held in view of all the prisoners, after evening roll call.

September 8, 1943 – a transport of Jews arrived from the Theresienstadt ghetto-camp. They were placed in Birkenau sector BIIb, named the Famielienlager – Theresienstadt. The camp was liquidated in two stages in March and July 1944.

November 11, 1943 – Arthur Liebehenschel succeeded Rudolf Höss as commandant of Auschwitz.

November 22, 1943 - Auschwitz divided into three autonomous concentration camps: Auschwitz I – Stammlager (the main camp); Auschwitz II-Birkenau; and Auschwitz III- Aussenlager.

May 1944 – the extermination of the Hungarian Jews begins. More than 400 thousand Jews arrive through July, the majority of whom are murdered in the as chambers.

August 2, 1944 – liquidation of the Gypsy family camp in Birkenau, Zigeunerlager.

August 12, 1944 – the first transport of civilians arrested on a mass scale after the start of the Warsaw Uprising arrived in Auschwitz II-Birkenau.

October 7, 1944 – mutiny by members of the Sonderkommando, resulting in the destruction of crematorium IV.

January 17, 1945 – the final roll call in Auschwitz-Birkenau.

January 17-18, 1945 – the start of the evacuation march. After three days, the majority of approximately 60 thousand prisoners arrived on foot in Wodzisław Śląski and Gliwice, from where trains carried them to concentration camps in the depths of Germany.

January 27, 1945 – the liberation of Auschwitz by the Soviet army.

Bibliography

If you are interested in this subject, you can find more information about medical experiments at Auschwitz in the scholarly literature and memoirs. Here are some suggestions:

Fejkiel Władysław, *Eksperymenty dokonywane przez personel sanitarny SS w głównym obozie koncentracyjnym w Oświęcimiu*, „Przegląd Lekarski – Oświęcim", Kraków 1964, nr 1, pp. 101–105.

Fejkiel Władysław, *Etyczno-prawne granice eksperymentowania w medycynie a sprawa profesora Clauberga*, Zeszyty Oświęcimskie, Oświęcim 1958 nr 2, pp.23 –39.

Fejkiel Władysław, *Medycyna za drutami, (in:) Pamiętniki lekarzy*, Warszawa 1968.

Fejkiel Władysław, *O służbie zdrowia w obozie koncentracyjnym w Oświęcimiu I (obóz główny)*, „Przegląd Lekarski – Oświęcim", Kraków 1961, nr 1a, pp. 44–51.

Głowacki Czesław, *Z dokumentacji zbrodniczych doświadczeń Carla Clauberga*, „Przegląd Lekarski – Oświęcim", Kraków 1976, nr 1, pp. 85–90.

Kaul Friedrich Karl, *Ärzte in Auschwitz*, Berlin 1968.

Kłodzinski Stanisław, *Zbrodnicze doświadczenia farmakologiczne na więźniach obozu koncentracyjnego w Oświęcimiu (Preparat 3582, rutenol, Be 1034, periston)*, „Przegląd Lekarski – Oświęcim", Kraków 1965, nr 1, pp. 40–46.

Kubica Helena, dr Mengele und seine Verbrechen im Konzentrationslager Auschwitz-Birkenau. Hefte von Auschwitz, Verlag Staatliches Muzeum Auschwitz – Birkenau 1997, nr 20, pp. 369–455.

Lasik Aleksander, *Edurad Wirths, Biuletyn Towarzystwa Opieki nad Oświęcimiem*, Warszawa 1993 nr 17, pp. 5–20.

Lasik Aleksander, die Personalbesetzung des Gesundheitsdienstes der SS im Konzentrationslager Auschwitz-Birkenau in den Jahren 1940–1945, Verlag Staatliches Muzeum Auschwitz – Birkenau 1997, nr 20, s. 290–368

Mikulski Jan, *Eksperymenty farmakologiczne w obozie koncentracyjnym Oświęcim – Brzezinka*, Zeszyty Oświęcimskie, Oświęcim 1967, nr 10, pp. 3–18.

Mikulski Jan, *Medycyna hitlerowska w służbie III Rzeszy*, Warszawa 1981.

Mitscherlich Aleksander, Mielke Fred, *Medizin ohne Menschlichkeit. Dokumente des Nürnberger Ärzteprozesses*, Frankfurt am Main 2004.

Nyiszli Miklós, *Pracownia doktora Mengele*, Warszawa 1966.

Schabel Reimund, Macht ohne Moral. Eine dokumentation über die SS. Frankfurt a. Mein 1957, pp. 276–283.

Schlesak Dieter, *Capesius der Auschwitzapotheker*, Bonn 2006.

Sehn Jan, *Sprawa oświęcimskiego lekarza SS J. P. Kremera.* „Przegląd Lekarski – Oświęcim", Kraków 1962. nr 1a, pp. 49–61.

Sehn Jan, *Carl Claubergs verbrecherische Unfruchtbarmachungs – Versuche an Häftlings-Frauen in den Nazi – Konzentationslagern,* Hefte von Auschwitz, Verlag Staatliches Muzeum Auschwitz – Birkenau 1997, nr 2, pp. 3–32.

Sterkowicz Stanisław, *Zbrodnicze eksperymenty medyczne w obozach koncentracyjnych Trzeciej Rzeszy,* Warszawa 1981.

Strzelecka Irena, *Experiments,* (in:) *Auschwitz. Nazi Death Camp,* Oświęcim 1996, pp. 88–102.

Table of Contents